S0-BZP-843

EYEWITNESS VISUAL DICTIONARIES

THE VISUAL
DICTIONARY *of*
CARS

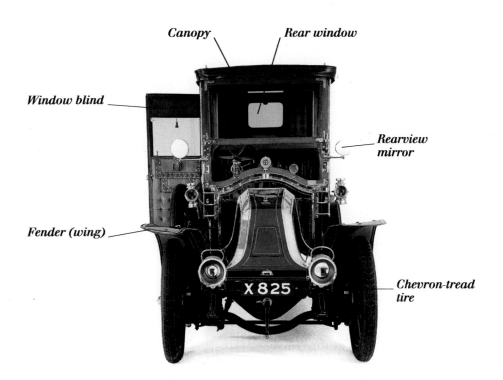

Canopy

Rear window

Window blind

Rearview mirror

Fender (wing)

Chevron-tread tire

X 825

FRONT VIEW OF 1906 RENAULT

PROPERTY OF
THE ISLAMIC ACADEMY
125 OAKLAND AVE.
METHUEN MA 01844

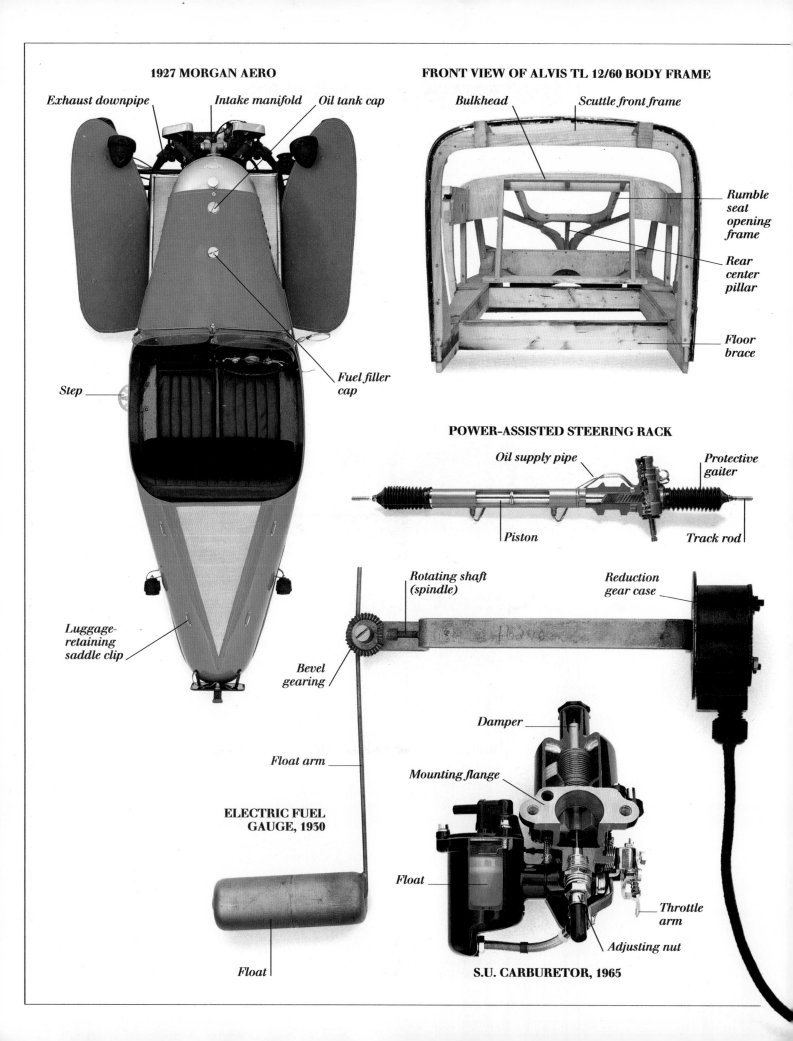

1927 MORGAN AERO

Exhaust downpipe
Intake manifold
Oil tank cap
Step
Fuel filler cap
Luggage-retaining saddle clip

FRONT VIEW OF ALVIS TL 12/60 BODY FRAME

Bulkhead
Scuttle front frame
Rumble seat opening frame
Rear center pillar
Floor brace

POWER-ASSISTED STEERING RACK

Oil supply pipe
Protective gaiter
Piston
Track rod

Rotating shaft (spindle)
Reduction gear case
Bevel gearing

Float arm

ELECTRIC FUEL GAUGE, 1930

Damper
Mounting flange
Float
Throttle arm
Adjusting nut

Float

S.U. CARBURETOR, 1965

EYEWITNESS VISUAL DICTIONARIES

THE VISUAL
DICTIONARY *of*
CARS

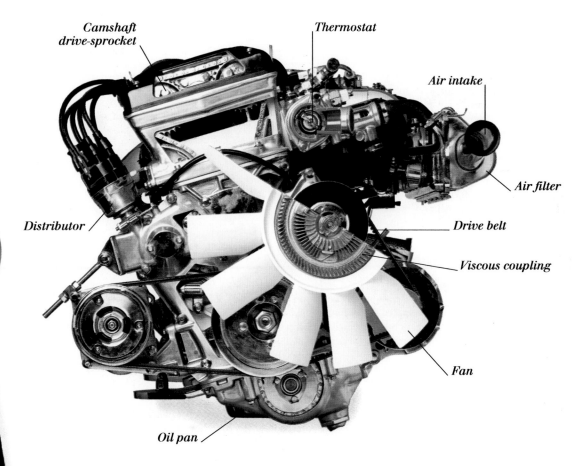

Camshaft
drive-sprocket

Thermostat

Air intake

Indicator
needle

PETROL

GALLONS

Distributor

Air filter

Drive belt

Viscous coupling

Fan

Oil pan

Drive
cable

FRONT VIEW OF A JAGUAR STRAIGHT SIX ENGINE

SCHOLASTIC INC.
New York Toronto London Auckland Sydney
Mexico City New Delhi Hong Kong

PROJECT ART EDITOR NICOLA LIDDIARD
DESIGNER PAUL CALVER

PROJECT EDITOR PAUL DOCHERTY
CONSULTANT EDITOR DAVID BURGESS-WISE
U.S. CONSULTANT JONATHAN A. STEIN
U.S. EDITOR CHARLES WILLS

SERIES ART EDITOR STEPHEN KNOWLDEN
SERIES EDITOR MARTYN PAGE
ART DIRECTOR CHEZ PICTHALL
MANAGING EDITOR RUTH MIDGLEY

PHOTOGRAPHY SIMON CLAY, JOHN LEPINE, TIM RIDLEY, DAVE RUDKIN
ILLUSTRATIONS MICK GILLAH

PRODUCTION HILARY STEPHENS

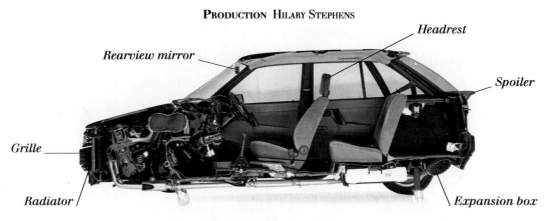

Rearview mirror — *Headrest* — *Spoiler*

Grille — *Radiator* — *Expansion box*

SECTIONED SEAT IBIZA

No part of this publication may be reproduced in whole or in part, or stored in a retrieval system, or transmitted in any form or by any means, electronic, mechanical, photocopying, recording, or otherwise, without written permission of the publisher. For information regarding permission, write to DK Publishing, Inc., 95 Madison Avenue, New York, NY 10016.

ISBN 0-439-11770-4

Copyright © 1992 by Dorling Kindersley Limited, London.
All rights reserved. Published by Scholastic Inc., 555 Broadway, New York, NY 10012, by arrangement with DK Publishing, Inc.

SCHOLASTIC and associated logos are trademarks and/or registered trademarks of Scholastic Inc.

12 11 10 9 8 7 6 5 4 3 2   9/9 0 1 2 3 4/0

Printed in the U.S.A.   14
First Scholastic printing, September 1999

Contents

Folding windshield

Honeycomb radiator

Beam axle

1913 ROLLS ROYCE SILVER GHOST TOURER

Gearbox

Fuel tank

1932 15/18 HP LANCHESTER RUNNING CHASSIS

Canvas tire

Felloe

Spoke

Hub

ARTILLERY WHEEL (WOODEN-SPOKED WHEEL)

THE FIRST CARS 6

ELEGANCE AND UTILITY 8

MASS PRODUCTION 10

THE "PEOPLE'S CAR" 12

EARLY ENGINES 14

MODERN ENGINES 16

ALTERNATIVE ENGINES 18

CARBURETORS 20

IGNITION SYSTEMS 22

POWER BOOSTERS 24

COOLING AND LUBRICATION 26

CLUTCH AND GEARBOX 28

TRANSMISSION SYSTEMS 30

FINAL DRIVE AND STEERING 32

SUSPENSION 34

WHEELS AND TIRES 36

BRAKES 38

INSTRUMENTS 40

ELECTRICAL SYSTEMS 42

MODERN BODYWORK 44

MODERN COMPONENTS 46

MODERN TRIM 48

COACHBUILT CARS 50

CARS ASSEMBLED BY HAND 52

TRIM AND UPHOLSTERY 54

ALL-TERRAIN VEHICLES 56

RACING CARS 58

INDEX 60

ACKNOWLEDGMENTS 64

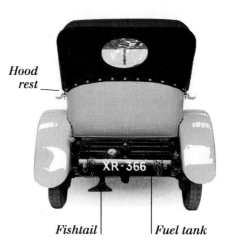

Hood rest

Fishtail

Fuel tank

1924 ROLLS ROYCE SILVER GHOST TOURER

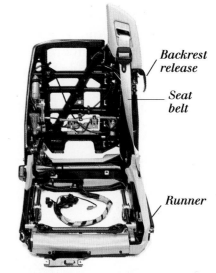

Backrest release

Seat belt

Runner

COMPUTERIZED ELECTRIC SEAT

Calorimeter

Radiator cap

Radiator badge

1973 ALFA ROMEO RADIATOR AND GRILLE

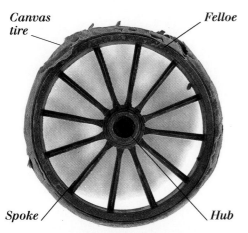

The first cars

THE EARLIEST ROAD VEHICLE powered by an engine, the Cugnot steam traction engine, was built in 1770. More practical steam carriages, such as the Bordino, were available in the early 19th century, but they were heavy and cumbersome. Restrictive laws and the introduction of railways, faster and able to carry more passengers, saw the decline of "cars" powered by steam. It was not until 1860 that the first practical power unit for road vehicles was developed with the invention of the internal combustion engine by the Belgian Étienne Lenoir. By around 1890, Karl Benz and Gottlieb Daimler in Germany and Albert de Dion and Armand Peugeot in France were building cars for sale to the public. These early cars, despite being primitive, expensive, and produced in limited numbers, heralded the age of the automobile.

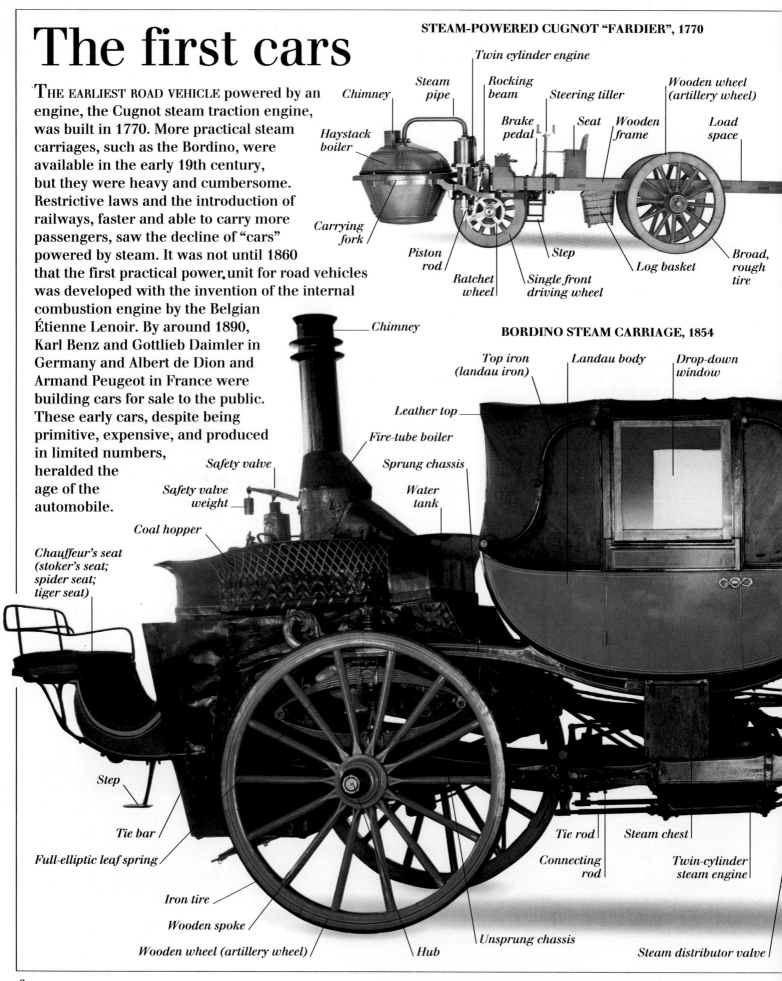

STEAM-POWERED CUGNOT "FARDIER", 1770

Chimney

Steam pipe

Twin cylinder engine

Rocking beam

Steering tiller

Brake pedal

Seat

Wooden frame

Wooden wheel (artillery wheel)

Load space

Haystack boiler

Carrying fork

Piston rod

Ratchet wheel

Single front driving wheel

Step

Log basket

Broad, rough tire

BORDINO STEAM CARRIAGE, 1854

Chimney

Top iron (landau iron)

Landau body

Drop-down window

Leather top

Fire-tube boiler

Sprung chassis

Water tank

Safety valve

Safety valve weight

Coal hopper

Chauffeur's seat (stoker's seat; spider seat; tiger seat)

Step

Tie bar

Full-elliptic leaf spring

Iron tire

Wooden spoke

Wooden wheel (artillery wheel)

Hub

Unsprung chassis

Tie rod

Connecting rod

Steam chest

Twin-cylinder steam engine

Steam distributor valve

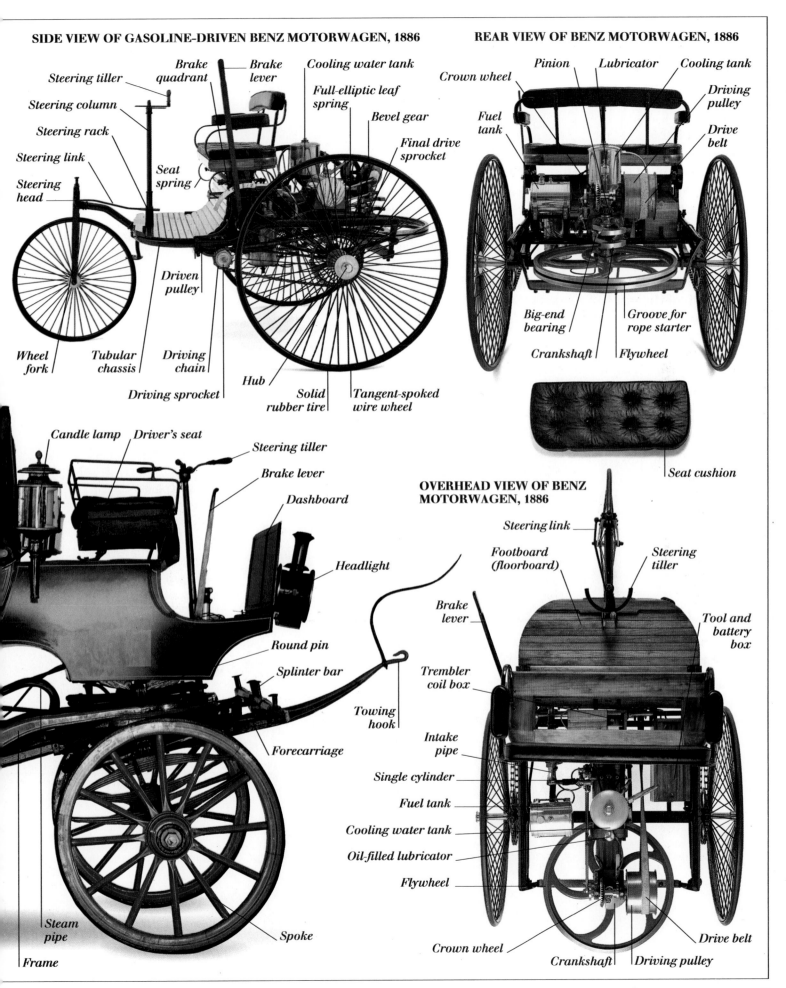

SIDE VIEW OF GASOLINE-DRIVEN BENZ MOTORWAGEN, 1886

Steering tiller
Brake quadrant
Brake lever
Cooling water tank
Steering column
Full-elliptic leaf spring
Steering rack
Bevel gear
Steering link
Final drive sprocket
Steering head
Seat spring
Driven pulley
Wheel fork
Tubular chassis
Driving chain
Driving sprocket
Hub
Solid rubber tire
Tangent-spoked wire wheel

REAR VIEW OF BENZ MOTORWAGEN, 1886

Pinion
Lubricator
Cooling tank
Crown wheel
Driving pulley
Fuel tank
Drive belt
Big-end bearing
Groove for rope starter
Crankshaft
Flywheel
Seat cushion

Candle lamp
Driver's seat
Steering tiller
Brake lever
Dashboard
Headlight
Round pin
Splinter bar
Towing hook
Forecarriage
Steam pipe
Spoke
Frame

OVERHEAD VIEW OF BENZ MOTORWAGEN, 1886

Steering link
Footboard (floorboard)
Steering tiller
Brake lever
Tool and battery box
Trembler coil box
Intake pipe
Single cylinder
Fuel tank
Cooling water tank
Oil-filled lubricator
Flywheel
Crown wheel
Crankshaft
Driving pulley
Drive belt

Elegance and utility

DURING THE FIRST DECADE OF THIS CENTURY, the motorist who could afford it had a choice of some of the finest cars ever made. These handbuilt cars were powerful and luxurious, using the finest wood, leather, and cloth, and bodywork made to the customer's individual requirements. Some had six-cylinder engines as big as 15 liters. The price of such cars was several times that of an average house, and their yearly running costs were also very high. As a result, basic, utilitarian cars became popular. Costing perhaps one-tenth of the price of a luxury car, these cars had very little trim and often had only single-cylinder engines.

1904 OLDSMOBILE SINGLE-CYLINDER ENGINE

Oil bottle dripfeed — Crankcase — Starting handle bracket — Exhaust pipe — Cylinder head — Cylinder — Starter cog — Carburetor — Engine timing gear — Crankshaft — Flywheel — Gear band

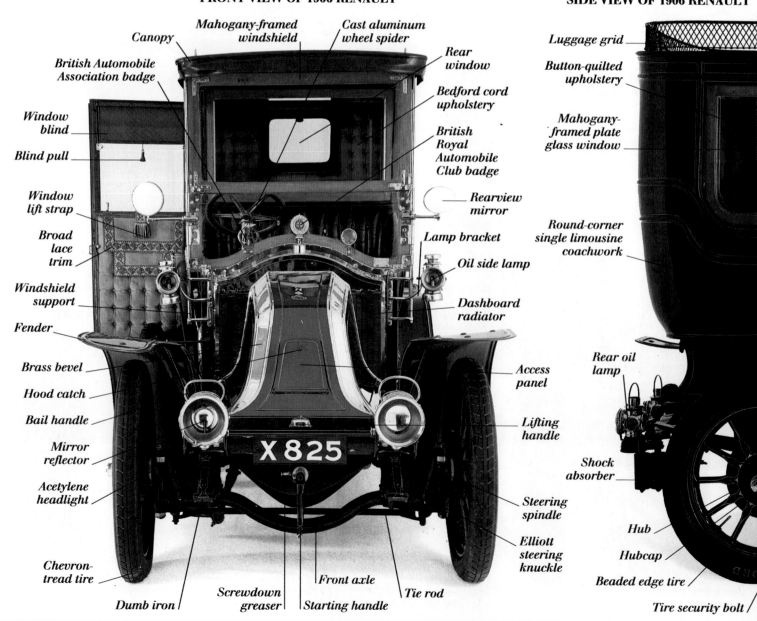

FRONT VIEW OF 1906 RENAULT

Canopy — Mahogany-framed windshield — Cast aluminum wheel spider — Rear window — British Automobile Association badge — Bedford cord upholstery — British Royal Automobile Club badge — Window blind — Blind pull — Window lift strap — Rearview mirror — Broad lace trim — Lamp bracket — Windshield support — Oil side lamp — Fender — Dashboard radiator — Brass bevel — Hood catch — Access panel — Bail handle — Lifting handle — Mirror reflector — Acetylene headlight — Steering spindle — Elliott steering knuckle — Chevron-tread tire — Dumb iron — Screwdown greaser — Front axle — Starting handle — Tie rod

SIDE VIEW OF 1906 RENAULT

Luggage grid — Button-quilted upholstery — Mahogany-framed plate glass window — Round-corner single limousine coachwork — Rear oil lamp — Shock absorber — Hub — Hubcap — Beaded edge tire — Tire security bolt

X 825

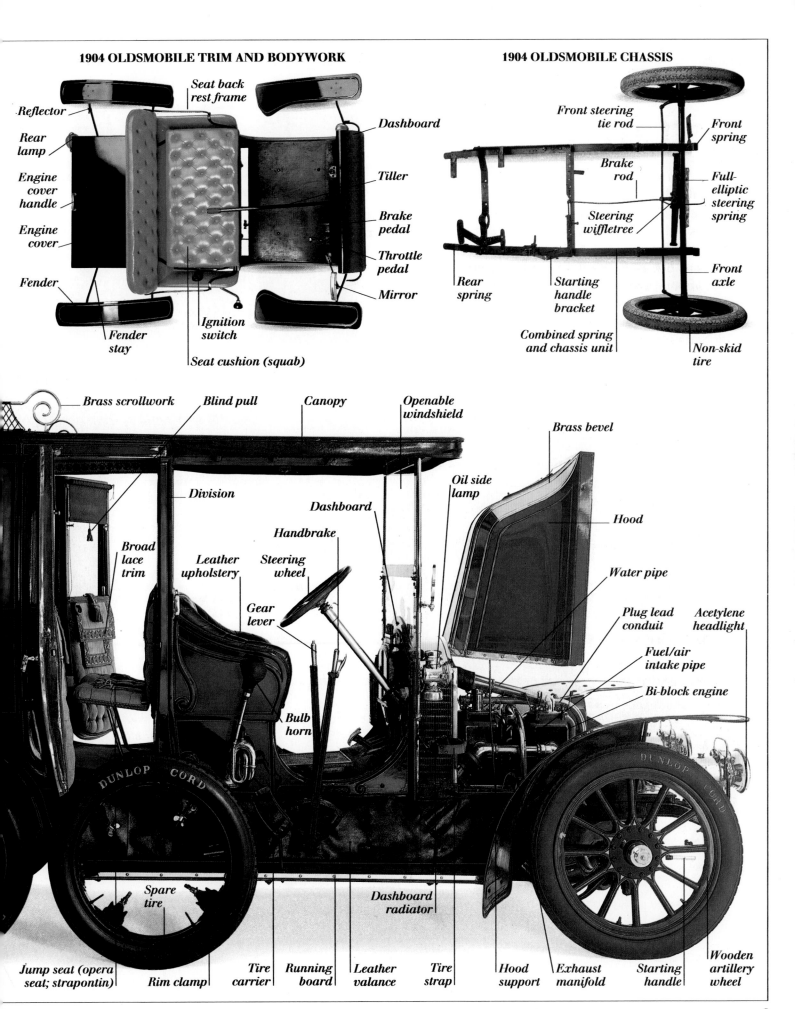

1904 OLDSMOBILE TRIM AND BODYWORK

Reflector
Rear lamp
Engine cover handle
Engine cover
Fender
Fender stay
Seat back rest frame
Ignition switch
Seat cushion (squab)
Dashboard
Tiller
Brake pedal
Throttle pedal
Mirror

1904 OLDSMOBILE CHASSIS

Front steering tie rod
Front spring
Brake rod
Full-elliptic steering spring
Steering wiffletree
Rear spring
Starting handle bracket
Combined spring and chassis unit
Front axle
Non-skid tire

Brass scrollwork
Blind pull
Canopy
Openable windshield
Brass bevel
Oil side lamp
Division
Dashboard
Hood
Broad lace trim
Handbrake
Leather upholstery
Steering wheel
Water pipe
Plug lead conduit
Acetylene headlight
Gear lever
Fuel/air intake pipe
Bi-block engine
Bulb horn
Spare tire
Dashboard radiator
Jump seat (opera seat; strapontin)
Rim clamp
Tire carrier
Running board
Leather valance
Tire strap
Hood support
Exhaust manifold
Starting handle
Wooden artillery wheel

Mass production

THE FIRST CARS WERE HAND-ASSEMBLED from individually built parts, a time-consuming procedure that required skilled mechanics and made cars very expensive. This problem was solved, in America, by a Detroit car manufacturer named Henry Ford. He introduced mass production by using standardized parts, and later combined these with a moving production line. The work was brought to the workers, each of whom performed one simple task in the construction process as the chassis moved along the line. The first mass-produced car, the Ford Model T, was launched in 1908. At first it was available in a limited range of body styles and colors. However, when the production line was introduced in 1914, the color range was cut back; the Model T became available, as Henry Ford said, in "any color you like, so long as it's black." Ford cut the production time for a car from several days to about 12 hours, and eventually to minutes, making cars much cheaper than before. As a result, half the cars in the world were Model T Fords by 1920.

FRONT VIEW OF 1913 FORD MODEL T

Throttle lever
Openable windshield
Steering wheel
Ignition lever
Windshield stay
Dashboard
Side lamp
Spring shock absorber
Bulb horn
Fender
Headlight
Radiator
Front transverse leaf spring
Front axle
License plate
Starting handle
Steering knuckle
Steering spindle connecting-rod

STAGES OF FORD MODEL T PRODUCTION

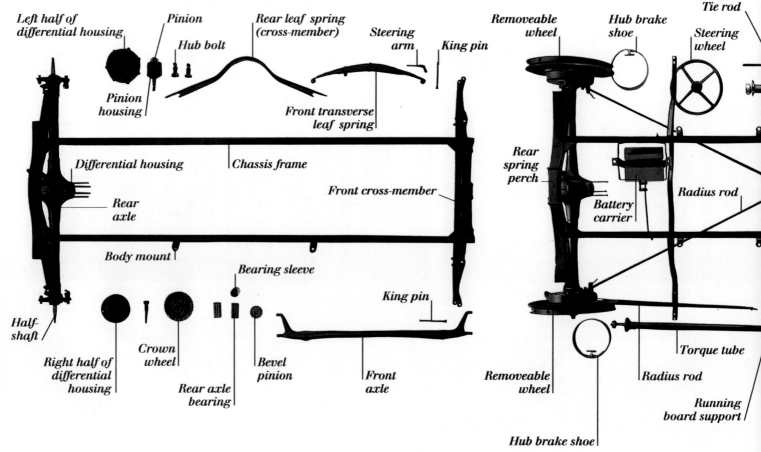

Left half of differential housing
Pinion
Rear leaf spring (cross-member)
Steering arm
King pin
Removeable wheel
Hub brake shoe
Tie rod
Steering wheel
Hub bolt
Pinion housing
Front transverse leaf spring
Differential housing
Chassis frame
Front cross-member
Rear spring perch
Battery carrier
Radius rod
Rear axle
Body mount
Bearing sleeve
King pin
Half-shaft
Right half of differential housing
Crown wheel
Rear axle bearing
Bevel pinion
Front axle
Removeable wheel
Radius rod
Torque tube
Running board support
Hub brake shoe

SIDE VIEW OF 1913 FORD MODEL T

Top

Rear seat

Top frame

Front seat

Steering wheel

Steering column

Windshield

Side lamp

Hood

Radiator filler cap

Radiator filler neck

Front fender

Spring shock absorber

Rear door

Horn bulb

Rear fender

Tire valve

Drain plug

Horn

Wooden-spoked wheel

Hub cap

Running board

Valance

Spare tire

Dummy front door

Radius rod

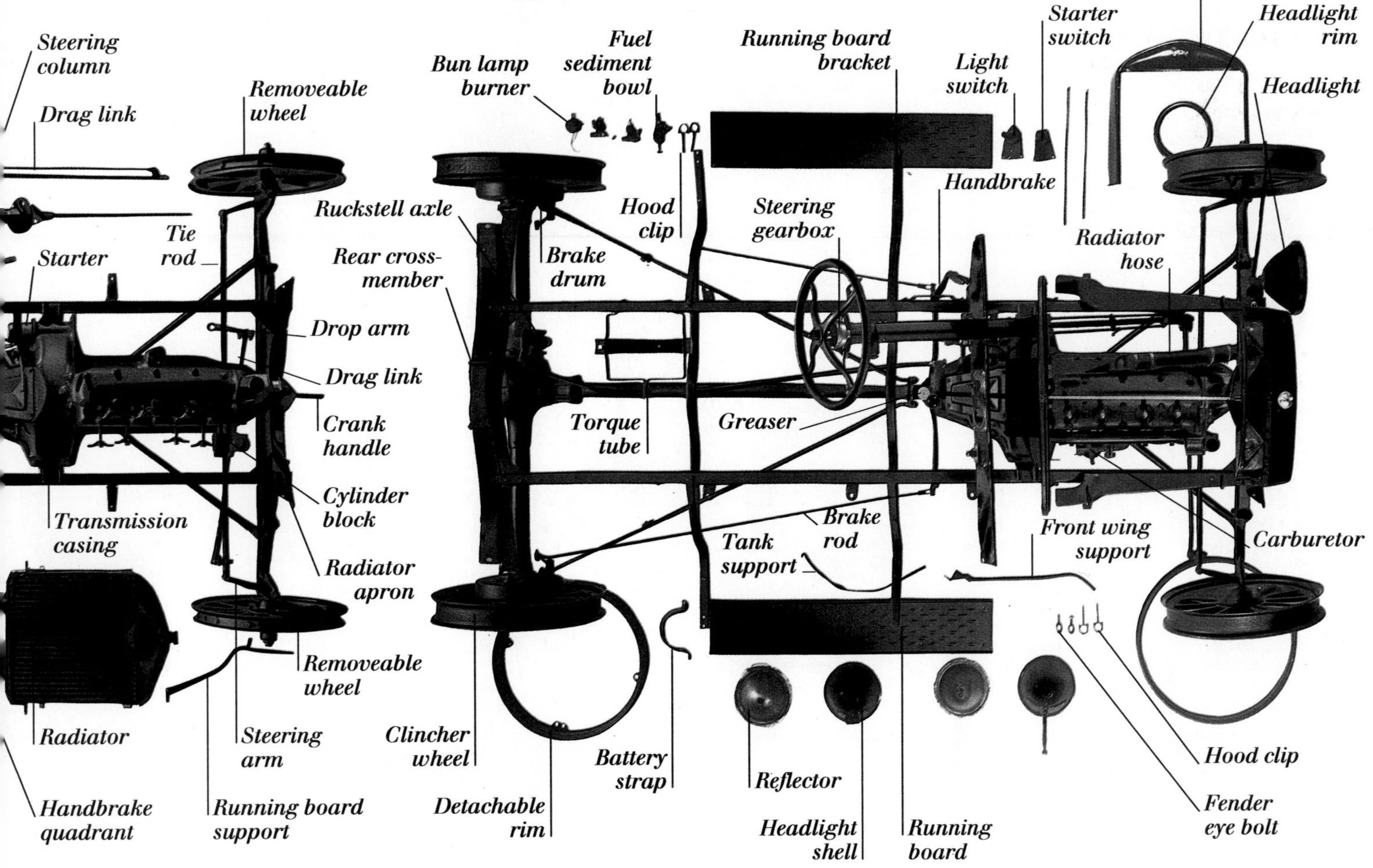

Radiator shell

Steering column

Drag link

Removeable wheel

Bun lamp burner

Fuel sediment bowl

Running board bracket

Light switch

Starter switch

Handbrake

Headlight rim

Headlight

Ruckstell axle

Hood clip

Steering gearbox

Radiator hose

Tie rod

Starter

Rear cross-member

Brake drum

Drop arm

Drag link

Crank handle

Cylinder block

Torque tube

Greaser

Transmission casing

Brake rod

Front wing support

Carburetor

Tank support

Radiator apron

Radiator

Removeable wheel

Steering arm

Clincher wheel

Battery strap

Reflector

Hood clip

Fender eye bolt

Handbrake quadrant

Running board support

Detachable rim

Headlight shell

Running board

11

The "people's car"

THE MOST POPULAR CAR in the history of car manufacture is the Volkswagen Beetle, originally called the KdF Wagen. The car was developed in Germany in the 1930s by Dr. Ferdinand Porsche. At that time, Germany had only half the number of cars of Britain or France, and Adolf Hitler took a personal interest in the development of the Volkswagen ("people's car"). The intention was to provide a new industry, new jobs, and a car so inexpensive that anyone with a job could afford it. Dr. Porsche designed a car that was cheap to build and run; its rear-mounted, air-cooled engine cut down the number of parts needed and also reduced weight. However, few civilians managed to obtain the Beetle before the outbreak of the Second World War in 1939. After the war, the Beetle proved so popular that eventually more than 20 million were sold.

CUSTOMIZED VOLKSWAGEN BEETLE

FLAT-FOUR CYLINDER ARRANGEMENT

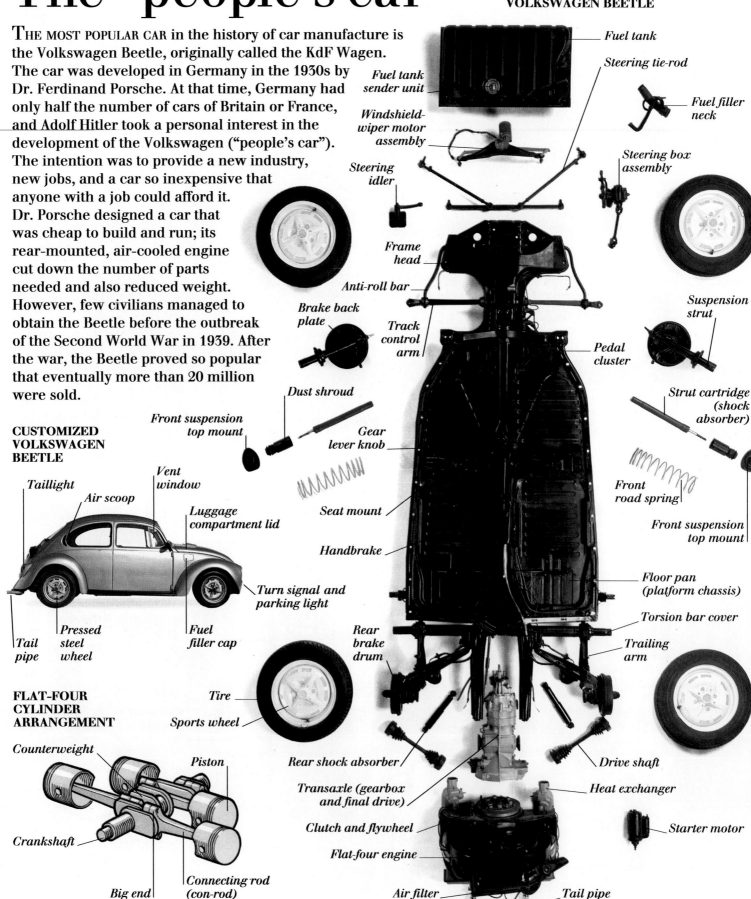

Fuel tank

Steering tie-rod

Fuel filler neck

Fuel tank sender unit

Windshield-wiper motor assembly

Steering box assembly

Steering idler

Frame head

Anti-roll bar

Suspension strut

Track control arm

Pedal cluster

Brake back plate

Strut cartridge (shock absorber)

Dust shroud

Front suspension top mount

Gear lever knob

Front road spring

Seat mount

Front suspension top mount

Handbrake

Floor pan (platform chassis)

Torsion bar cover

Taillight

Vent window

Trailing arm

Air scoop

Luggage compartment lid

Rear brake drum

Turn signal and parking light

Tire

Pressed steel wheel

Fuel filler cap

Sports wheel

Tail pipe

Counterweight

Piston

Rear shock absorber

Drive shaft

Transaxle (gearbox and final drive)

Heat exchanger

Crankshaft

Clutch and flywheel

Starter motor

Flat-four engine

Big end

Connecting rod (con-rod)

Air filter

Tail pipe

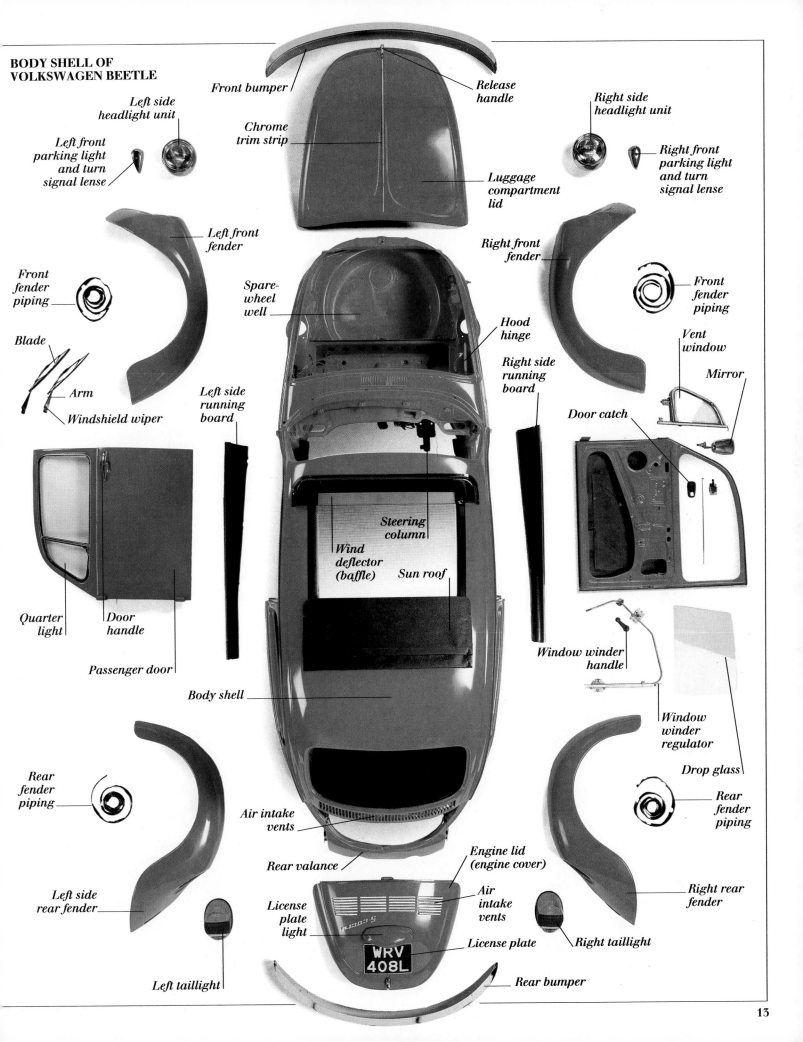

BODY SHELL OF VOLKSWAGEN BEETLE

Front bumper

Release handle

Left side headlight unit

Right side headlight unit

Left front parking light and turn signal lense

Chrome trim strip

Right front parking light and turn signal lense

Luggage compartment lid

Left front fender

Right front fender

Front fender piping

Spare-wheel well

Hood hinge

Front fender piping

Blade

Right side running board

Vent window

Arm

Left side running board

Mirror

Windshield wiper

Door catch

Wind deflector (baffle)

Steering column

Sun roof

Quarter light

Door handle

Passenger door

Window winder handle

Body shell

Window winder regulator

Drop glass

Rear fender piping

Rear fender piping

Air intake vents

Rear valance

Engine lid (engine cover)

Left side rear fender

Air intake vents

Right rear fender

Left taillight

License plate light

License plate

Right taillight

WRV 408L

Rear bumper

Early engines

STEAM AND ELECTRICITY were used to power cars until early this century, but neither power source was ideal. Electric cars had to stop frequently to recharge their heavy batteries, and steam cars gave smooth power delivery but were too complicated for the average motorist to use. A rival power source, the internal combustion engine, was invented in 1860 by Étienne Lenoir (see pp. 6-7). This engine converted the force of an explosion into rotary motion to turn the wheels of a vehicle. Early variations on this basic model included sleeve valves, separately cast cylinders, and the two-stroke combustion cycle. Today, all combustion engines, including the Wankel rotary and diesels (see pp. 18-19), use the four-stroke cycle, first demonstrated by Nikolaus Otto in 1876. The Otto cycle has proved the best method of ensuring that the engine turns over smoothly and that exhaust emissions are controllable.

TROJAN TWO-STROKE ENGINE, 1927

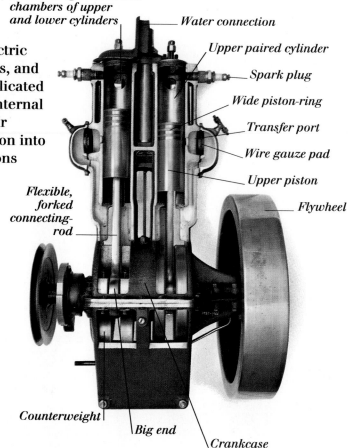

Port linking combustion chambers of upper and lower cylinders

Water connection

Upper paired cylinder

Spark plug

Wide piston-ring

Transfer port

Wire gauze pad

Upper piston

Flywheel

Flexible, forked connecting-rod

Counterweight

Big end

Crankcase

BERSEY ELECTRIC CAB, 1896

Mounting for tray of 40 batteries

Housing for electric motors

SECTIONED WHITE STEAM CAR, 1903

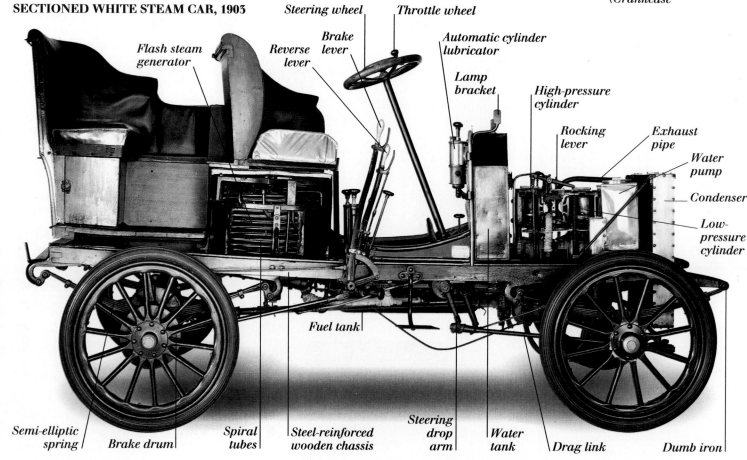

Flash steam generator

Reverse lever

Brake lever

Steering wheel

Throttle wheel

Automatic cylinder lubricator

Lamp bracket

High-pressure cylinder

Rocking lever

Exhaust pipe

Water pump

Condenser

Low-pressure cylinder

Fuel tank

Semi-elliptic spring

Brake drum

Spiral tubes

Steel-reinforced wooden chassis

Steering drop arm

Water tank

Drag link

Dumb iron

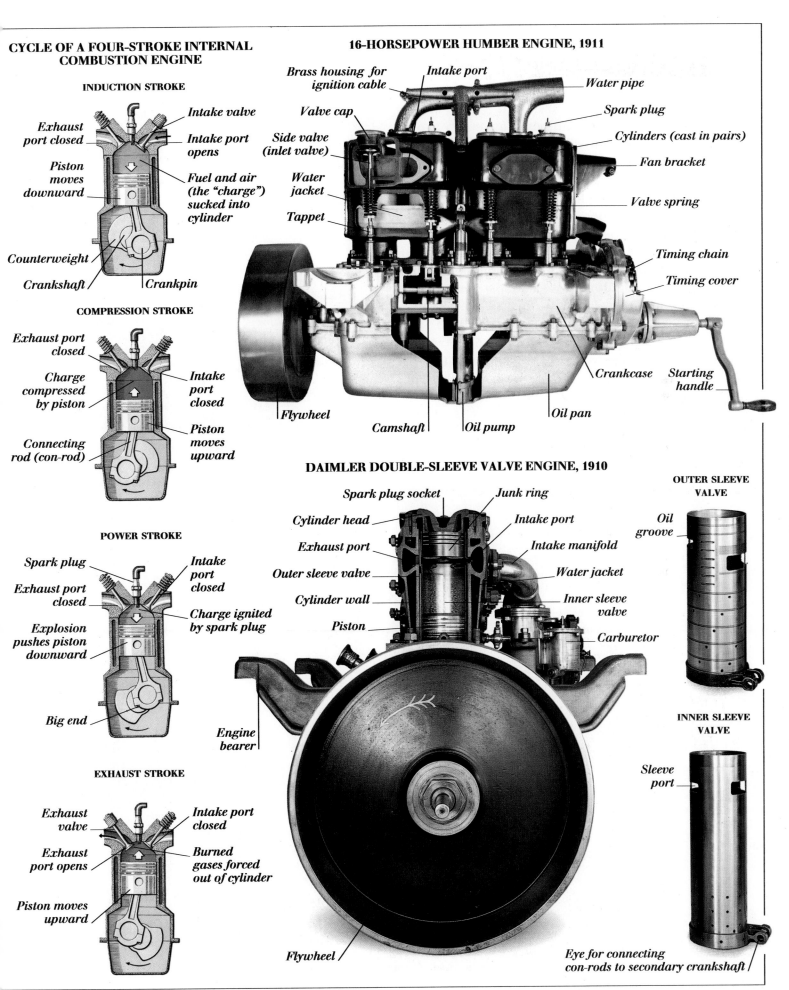

CYCLE OF A FOUR-STROKE INTERNAL COMBUSTION ENGINE

INDUCTION STROKE

Exhaust port closed
Piston moves downward
Counterweight
Crankshaft
Intake valve
Intake port opens
Fuel and air (the "charge") sucked into cylinder
Crankpin

COMPRESSION STROKE

Exhaust port closed
Charge compressed by piston
Connecting rod (con-rod)
Intake port closed
Piston moves upward

POWER STROKE

Spark plug
Exhaust port closed
Explosion pushes piston downward
Big end
Intake port closed
Charge ignited by spark plug

EXHAUST STROKE

Exhaust valve
Exhaust port opens
Piston moves upward
Intake port closed
Burned gases forced out of cylinder

16-HORSEPOWER HUMBER ENGINE, 1911

Brass housing for ignition cable
Intake port
Water pipe
Valve cap
Spark plug
Side valve (inlet valve)
Cylinders (cast in pairs)
Water jacket
Fan bracket
Tappet
Valve spring
Timing chain
Timing cover
Flywheel
Camshaft
Oil pump
Crankcase
Oil pan
Starting handle

DAIMLER DOUBLE-SLEEVE VALVE ENGINE, 1910

Spark plug socket
Junk ring
Cylinder head
Intake port
Exhaust port
Intake manifold
Outer sleeve valve
Water jacket
Cylinder wall
Inner sleeve valve
Piston
Carburetor
Engine bearer
Flywheel

OUTER SLEEVE VALVE

Oil groove

INNER SLEEVE VALVE

Sleeve port

Eye for connecting con-rods to secondary crankshaft

15

Modern engines

TODAY'S GASOLINE ENGINE WORKS on the same basic principles as the first car engines of a century ago, although it has been greatly refined. Modern engines, often made from special metal alloys, are much lighter than earlier engines. Computerized ignition systems (see pp. 22-23), fuel injectors (see pp. 24-25), and multi-valve cylinder heads achieve a more efficient combustion of the fuel/air mixture (the charge) so that less fuel is wasted. As a result of this greater efficiency, the power and performance of a modern engine are increased, and the level of pollution in the exhaust gases is reduced. Exhaust pollution levels today are also lowered by the increasing use of special filters called catalytic converters which absorb many exhaust pollutants. The need to produce ever more efficient engines means that it can take up to seven years to develop a new engine for a family car, at a cost of many millions of dollars.

FRONT VIEW OF A FORD COSWORTH V6 12-VALVE

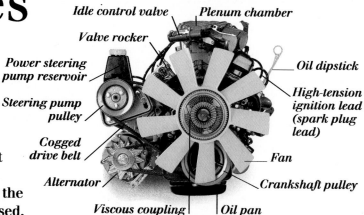

Idle control valve
Plenum chamber
Valve rocker
Power steering pump reservoir
Oil dipstick
High-tension ignition lead (spark plug lead)
Steering pump pulley
Cogged drive belt
Fan
Alternator
Crankshaft pulley
Viscous coupling
Oil pan

FRONT VIEW OF A FORD COSWORTH V6 24-VALVE

Idle control valve
Plenum chamber
Exhaust gas recirculation valve
Camshaft timing gear
Steering pump drive pulley
Camshaft chain
Belt tensioner
Air conditioning compressor
Alternator cooling fan
Oil pan
Drive belt
Crankshaft pulley

SECTIONED VIEW OF A JAGUAR STRAIGHT 6

Cam follower (bucket tappet)
Valve spring
Cam lobe
Cam
Combustion chamber
Compression ring
Cam cover
Camshaft
Distributor
Cylinder head
Fan
Valve stem
Air conditioning refrigerant pipe
Exhaust valve
Suspension self-levelling pump
Cylinder liner
Power steering pump
Water jacket
Piston
Swash plate
Connecting rod (con-rod)
Drive belt
Main bearing housing
Big end
Compressor piston
Transmission adaptor plate
Air conditioning compressor
Crankcase
Crankshaft counterweight
Oil pan
Oil pick-up pipe
Anti-surge baffle
Oil-control ring (scraper ring)

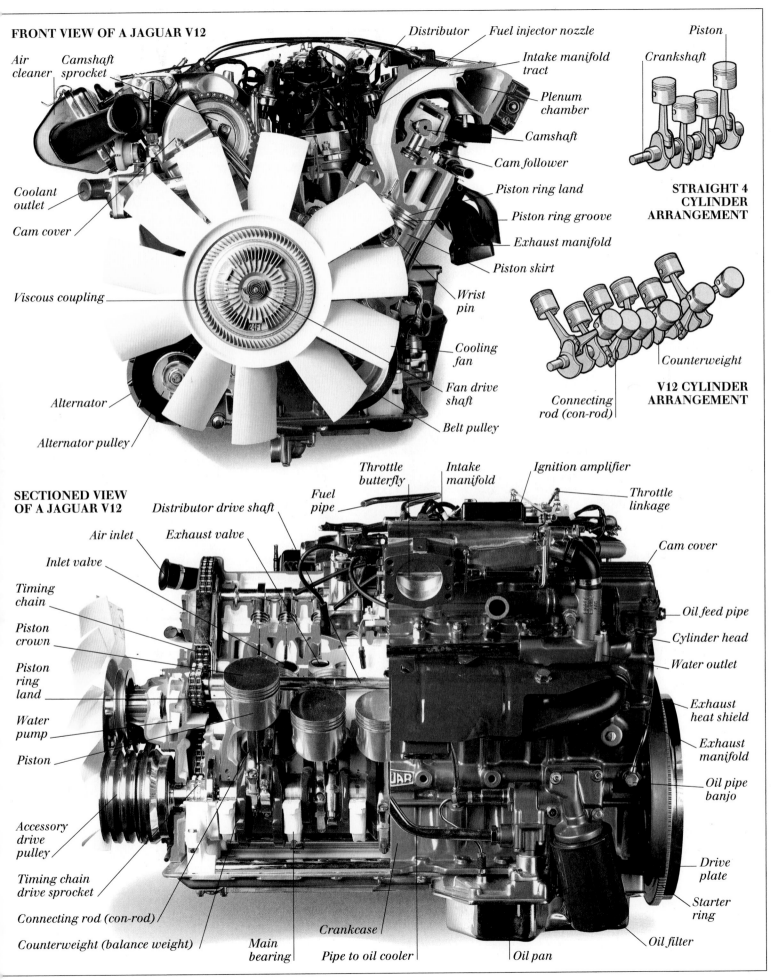

FRONT VIEW OF A JAGUAR V12

Air cleaner

Camshaft sprocket

Distributor

Fuel injector nozzle

Intake manifold tract

Plenum chamber

Camshaft

Cam follower

Piston ring land

Piston ring groove

Exhaust manifold

Piston skirt

Wrist pin

Coolant outlet

Cam cover

Viscous coupling

Cooling fan

Fan drive shaft

Alternator

Alternator pulley

Belt pulley

Piston

Crankshaft

STRAIGHT 4 CYLINDER ARRANGEMENT

Counterweight

Connecting rod (con-rod)

V12 CYLINDER ARRANGEMENT

SECTIONED VIEW OF A JAGUAR V12

Distributor drive shaft

Fuel pipe

Throttle butterfly

Intake manifold

Ignition amplifier

Throttle linkage

Air inlet

Exhaust valve

Inlet valve

Cam cover

Timing chain

Oil feed pipe

Piston crown

Cylinder head

Piston ring land

Water outlet

Water pump

Exhaust heat shield

Piston

Exhaust manifold

Oil pipe banjo

Accessory drive pulley

Timing chain drive sprocket

Connecting rod (con-rod)

Drive plate

Starter ring

Counterweight (balance weight)

Main bearing

Crankcase

Pipe to oil cooler

Oil pan

Oil filter

17

Alternative engines

THE MOST COMMON TYPE OF ALTERNATIVE ENGINE is the diesel engine. Instead of igniting the compressed fuel/air mixture with a spark, the diesel engine uses compression alone, which heats the mixture to the point where it explodes. A diesel engine's fuel consumption is low in comparison with similarly sized piston engines, despite its heavier, reinforced moving parts and cylinder block. Another type of engine is the rotary-combustion, first successfully developed by Felix Wankel in the 1950s. Its two trilobate (three-sided) rotors revolve in housings shaped in a fat figure eight. The four sequences of the four-stroke cycle, which occur consecutively in a piston engine, occur simultaneously in a rotary engine, producing power in a continuous stream.

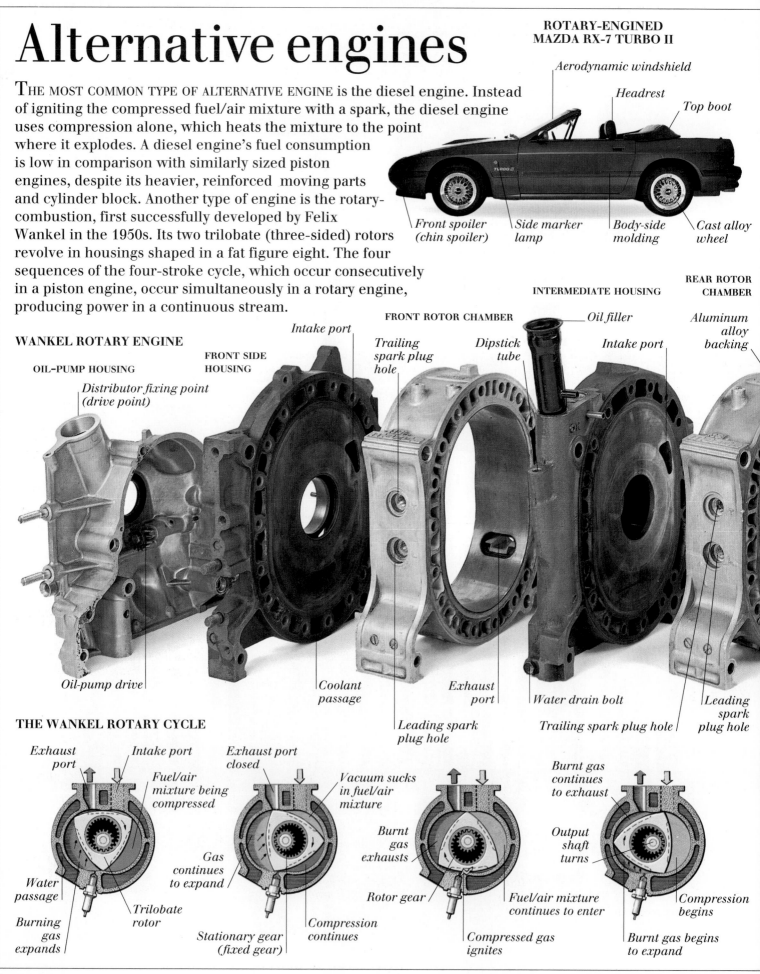

ROTARY-ENGINED MAZDA RX-7 TURBO II

- *Aerodynamic windshield*
- *Headrest*
- *Top boot*
- *Front spoiler (chin spoiler)*
- *Side marker lamp*
- *Body-side molding*
- *Cast alloy wheel*

WANKEL ROTARY ENGINE

- OIL-PUMP HOUSING
- *Distributor fixing point (drive point)*
- FRONT SIDE HOUSING
- *Intake port*
- FRONT ROTOR CHAMBER
- *Trailing spark plug hole*
- *Dipstick tube*
- *Oil filler*
- INTERMEDIATE HOUSING
- *Intake port*
- REAR ROTOR CHAMBER
- *Aluminum alloy backing*
- *Oil-pump drive*
- *Coolant passage*
- *Exhaust port*
- *Leading spark plug hole*
- *Water drain bolt*
- *Trailing spark plug hole*
- *Leading spark plug hole*

THE WANKEL ROTARY CYCLE

- *Exhaust port*
- *Intake port*
- *Fuel/air mixture being compressed*
- *Water passage*
- *Burning gas expands*
- *Trilobate rotor*

- *Exhaust port closed*
- *Vacuum sucks in fuel/air mixture*
- *Gas continues to expand*
- *Stationary gear (fixed gear)*
- *Compression continues*

- *Burnt gas exhausts*
- *Rotor gear*
- *Compressed gas ignites*
- *Fuel/air mixture continues to enter*

- *Burnt gas continues to exhaust*
- *Output shaft turns*
- *Burnt gas begins to expand*
- *Compression begins*

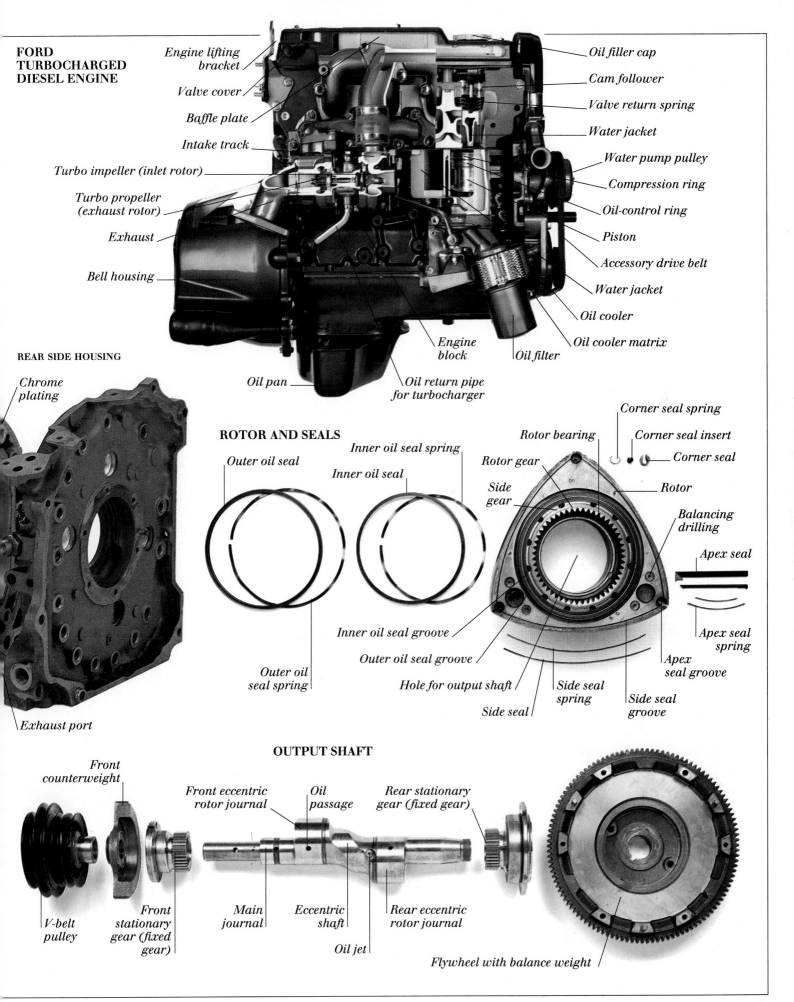

FORD TURBOCHARGED DIESEL ENGINE

Engine lifting bracket
Valve cover
Baffle plate
Intake track
Turbo impeller (inlet rotor)
Turbo propeller (exhaust rotor)
Exhaust
Bell housing

Oil filler cap
Cam follower
Valve return spring
Water jacket
Water pump pulley
Compression ring
Oil-control ring
Piston
Accessory drive belt
Water jacket
Oil cooler
Oil cooler matrix

Oil pan
Engine block
Oil return pipe for turbocharger
Oil filter

REAR SIDE HOUSING

Chrome plating

Exhaust port

ROTOR AND SEALS

Outer oil seal
Inner oil seal spring
Inner oil seal
Rotor bearing
Rotor gear
Side gear
Corner seal spring
Corner seal insert
Corner seal
Rotor
Balancing drilling
Apex seal

Inner oil seal groove
Outer oil seal groove
Outer oil seal spring
Hole for output shaft
Side seal spring
Side seal
Apex seal groove
Side seal groove
Apex seal spring

OUTPUT SHAFT

Front counterweight
Front eccentric rotor journal
Oil passage
Rear stationary gear (fixed gear)

V-belt pulley
Front stationary gear (fixed gear)
Main journal
Eccentric shaft
Rear eccentric rotor journal
Oil jet
Flywheel with balance weight

Carburetors

CARBURETORS MIX FUEL VAPOR AND AIR to create a gas (charge) that explodes when compressed and ignited in the engine cylinders. The fuel and air must be mixed in exactly the right proportions, which vary with speed and load, for the engine to work with maximum efficiency. The amount of air entering the carburetor is altered by opening and closing the throttle using the accelerator pedal. The air flows quickly as it enters a narrow passage called the venturi or choke. Here, the air passes over a narrow jet linked to a small fuel reservoir (the float chamber) and causes fuel to be sucked from the jet in a fine mist. Some carburetors vary the size of the venturi to control the amount of fuel and air; others the size of the fuel jets. Today, fuel injectors are increasingly replacing carburetors.

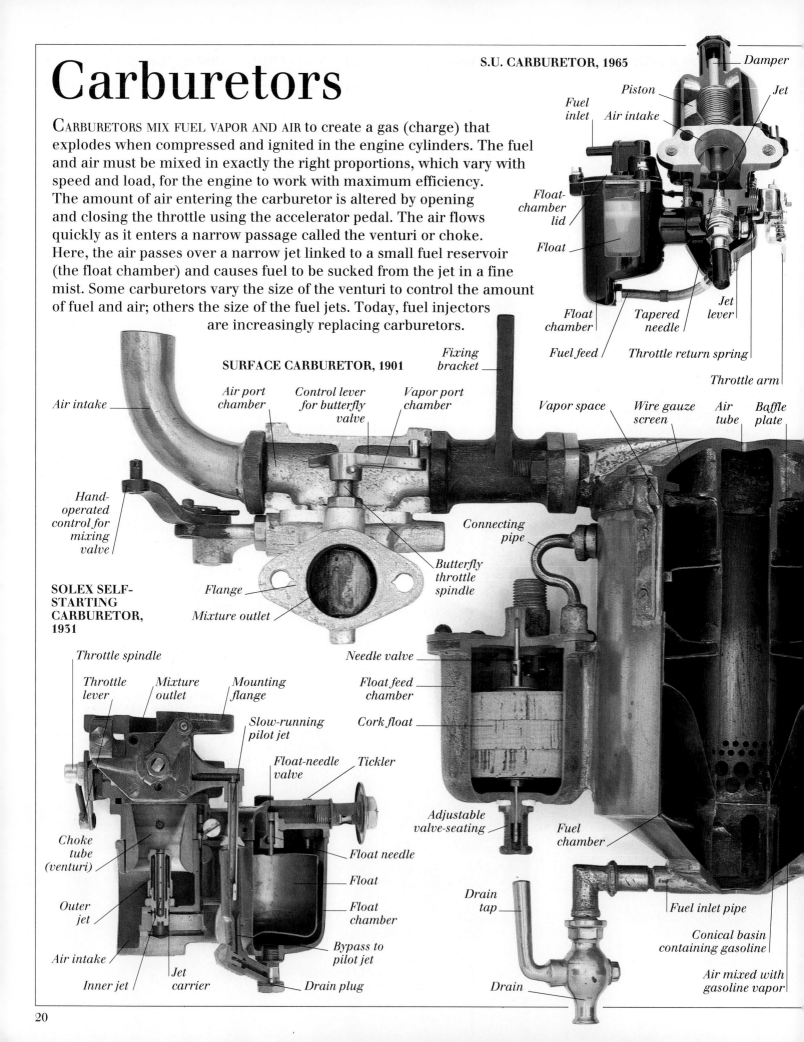

S.U. CARBURETOR, 1965

- Damper
- Piston
- Jet
- Fuel inlet
- Air intake
- Float-chamber lid
- Float
- Float chamber
- Tapered needle
- Jet lever
- Fuel feed
- Throttle return spring

SURFACE CARBURETOR, 1901

- Fixing bracket
- Air intake
- Air port chamber
- Control lever for butterfly valve
- Vapor port chamber
- Vapor space
- Wire gauze screen
- Air tube
- Baffle plate
- Throttle arm
- Hand-operated control for mixing valve
- Connecting pipe
- Butterfly throttle spindle
- Flange
- Mixture outlet
- Needle valve
- Float feed chamber
- Cork float
- Adjustable valve-seating
- Fuel chamber
- Drain tap
- Fuel inlet pipe
- Conical basin containing gasoline
- Drain
- Air mixed with gasoline vapor

SOLEX SELF-STARTING CARBURETOR, 1931

- Throttle spindle
- Throttle lever
- Mixture outlet
- Mounting flange
- Slow-running pilot jet
- Float-needle valve
- Tickler
- Choke tube (venturi)
- Outer jet
- Float needle
- Float
- Float chamber
- Air intake
- Inner jet
- Jet carrier
- Drain plug
- Bypass to pilot jet

WEBER TWIN CHOKE CARBURETOR, 1991

WEBER TWIN CHOKE CARBURETOR, 1991

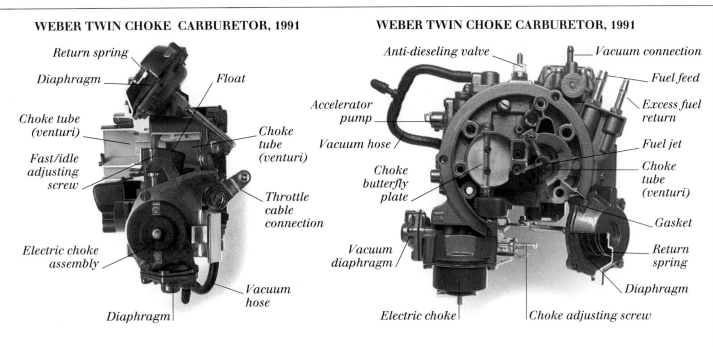

Return spring

Diaphragm

Choke tube (venturi)

Fast/idle adjusting screw

Electric choke assembly

Float

Choke tube (venturi)

Throttle cable connection

Vacuum hose

Diaphragm

Anti-dieseling valve

Vacuum connection

Accelerator pump

Fuel feed

Excess fuel return

Vacuum hose

Fuel jet

Choke butterfly plate

Choke tube (venturi)

Gasket

Vacuum diaphragm

Return spring

Diaphragm

Electric choke

Choke adjusting screw

SCOTT ROBINSON CARBURETOR, 1911

COX ATMOS CARBURETOR, 1918

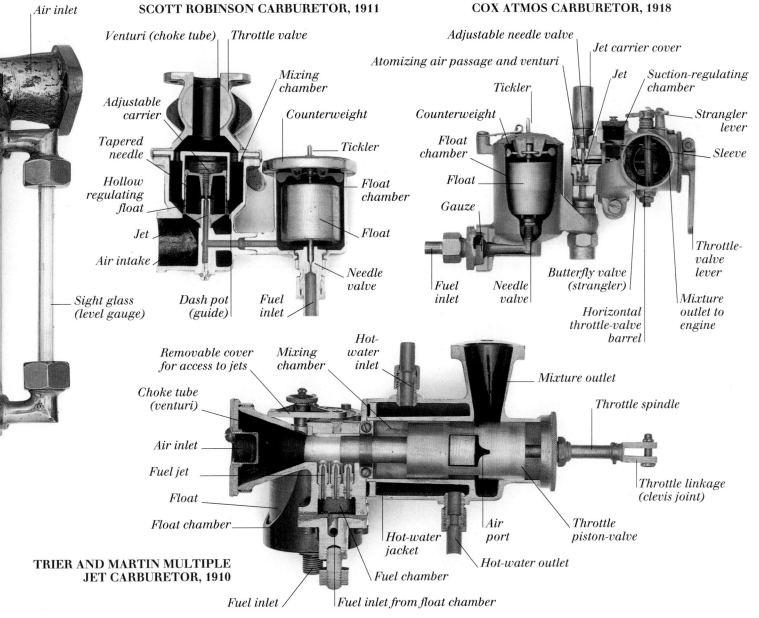

Air inlet

Venturi (choke tube)

Throttle valve

Mixing chamber

Adjustable carrier

Counterweight

Tapered needle

Tickler

Hollow regulating float

Float chamber

Jet

Float

Air intake

Needle valve

Sight glass (level gauge)

Dash pot (guide)

Fuel inlet

Adjustable needle valve

Jet carrier cover

Atomizing air passage and venturi

Jet

Suction-regulating chamber

Tickler

Counterweight

Strangler lever

Float chamber

Sleeve

Float

Gauze

Fuel inlet

Needle valve

Butterfly valve (strangler)

Horizontal throttle-valve barrel

Throttle-valve lever

Mixture outlet to engine

Removable cover for access to jets

Mixing chamber

Hot-water inlet

Mixture outlet

Choke tube (venturi)

Throttle spindle

Air inlet

Fuel jet

Float

Float chamber

Hot-water jacket

Air port

Throttle linkage (clevis joint)

Throttle piston-valve

Hot-water outlet

Fuel inlet

Fuel inlet from float chamber

Fuel chamber

TRIER AND MARTIN MULTIPLE JET CARBURETOR, 1910

Ignition systems

IGNITION OF THE FUEL/AIR MIXTURE in the engine must occur at precisely the moment of maximum compression to ensure the most efficient combustion. Some of the earliest cars used the crude method of red-hot platinum tubes heated by gasoline burners to ignite the mixture. Electric ignition soon took over: a distributor sent a carefully-timed electric current to each cylinder in turn, where the current jumped a gap between points in a spark plug, creating a spark to ignite the charge in the cylinder. Two favored methods of creating the current were the magneto, which generated a high-voltage electromagnetic current, and the coil, which amplified the voltage of a separate battery. Timing the spark might be performed mechanically by the distributor, or electronically by an electronic ignition system. The most modern systems use a computer to time the spark very precisely, allowing the engine to run at maximum efficiency.

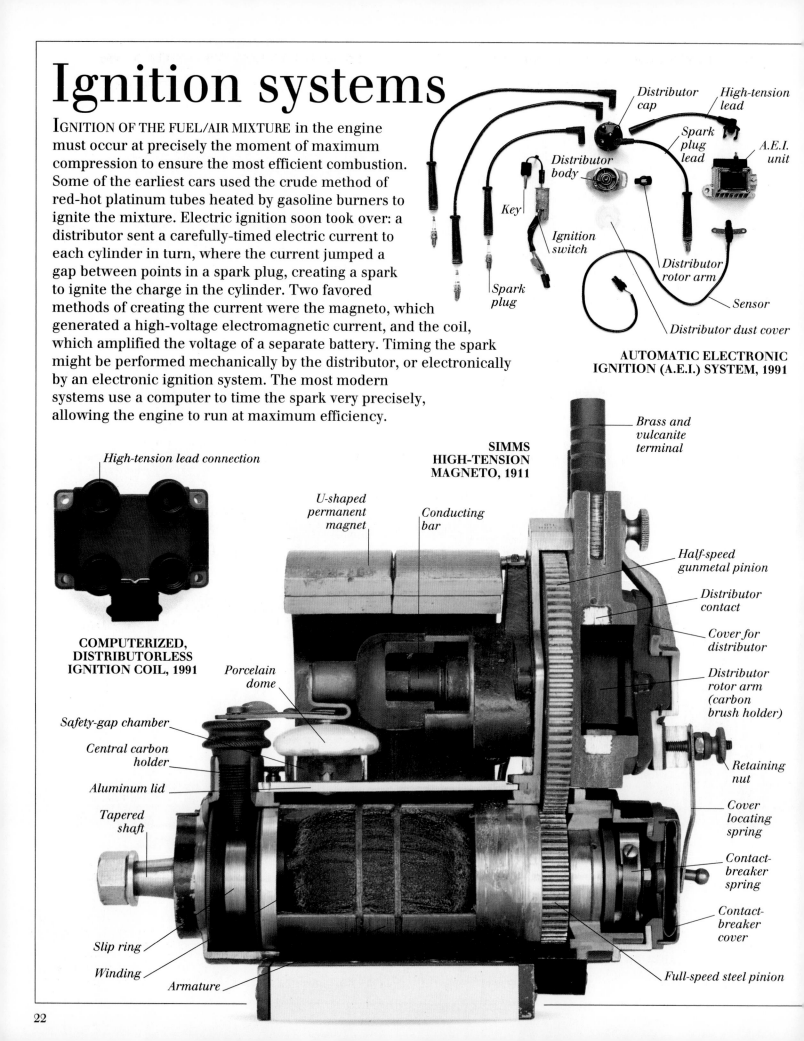

Distributor cap

High-tension lead

Spark plug lead

A.E.I. unit

Distributor body

Key

Ignition switch

Spark plug

Distributor rotor arm

Sensor

Distributor dust cover

AUTOMATIC ELECTRONIC IGNITION (A.E.I.) SYSTEM, 1991

High-tension lead connection

COMPUTERIZED, DISTRIBUTORLESS IGNITION COIL, 1991

SIMMS HIGH-TENSION MAGNETO, 1911

Brass and vulcanite terminal

U-shaped permanent magnet

Conducting bar

Half-speed gunmetal pinion

Distributor contact

Cover for distributor

Distributor rotor arm (carbon brush holder)

Porcelain dome

Safety-gap chamber

Central carbon holder

Aluminum lid

Tapered shaft

Retaining nut

Cover locating spring

Contact-breaker spring

Contact-breaker cover

Slip ring

Winding

Armature

Full-speed steel pinion

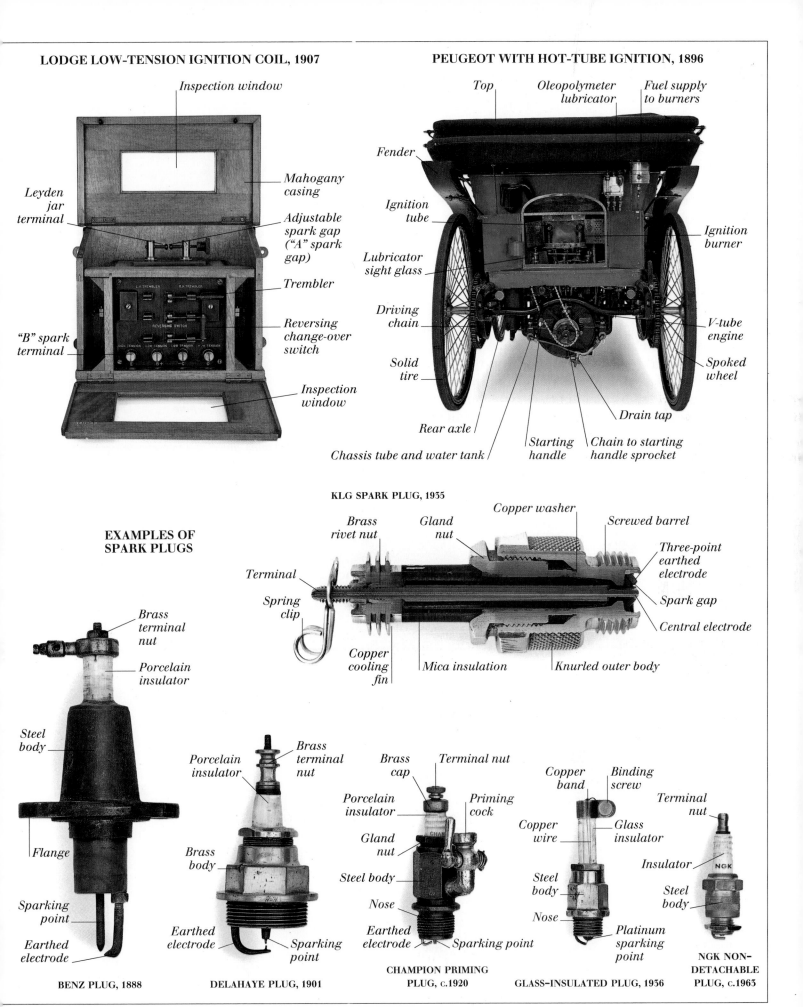

LODGE LOW-TENSION IGNITION COIL, 1907

Inspection window

Leyden jar terminal

Mahogany casing

Adjustable spark gap ("A" spark gap)

Trembler

Reversing change-over switch

"B" spark terminal

Inspection window

PEUGEOT WITH HOT-TUBE IGNITION, 1896

Top

Oleopolymeter lubricator

Fuel supply to burners

Fender

Ignition tube

Ignition burner

Lubricator sight glass

Driving chain

V-tube engine

Solid tire

Spoked wheel

Rear axle

Drain tap

Chassis tube and water tank

Starting handle

Chain to starting handle sprocket

KLG SPARK PLUG, 1935

Brass rivet nut

Gland nut

Copper washer

Screwed barrel

Terminal

Three-point earthed electrode

Spring clip

Spark gap

Central electrode

Copper cooling fin

Mica insulation

Knurled outer body

EXAMPLES OF SPARK PLUGS

Brass terminal nut

Porcelain insulator

Steel body

Flange

Sparking point

Earthed electrode

BENZ PLUG, 1888

Porcelain insulator

Brass terminal nut

Brass body

Earthed electrode

Sparking point

DELAHAYE PLUG, 1901

Brass cap

Terminal nut

Porcelain insulator

Priming cock

Gland nut

Steel body

Nose

Earthed electrode

Sparking point

CHAMPION PRIMING PLUG, c.1920

Copper band

Binding screw

Copper wire

Glass insulator

Steel body

Nose

Platinum sparking point

GLASS-INSULATED PLUG, 1936

Terminal nut

Insulator

Steel body

NGK NON-DETACHABLE PLUG, c.1963

23

Power boosters

AN ENGINE'S POWER OUTPUT can be increased by forcing more of the fuel/air mixture (the charge) into the cylinders (forced induction) to provide a bigger explosion on the power stroke. There are two types of forced induction: supercharging and turbocharging. A supercharger, or blower, uses rotating vanes or lobes to force air into the engine; the increased flow of air sucks (or blows) more fuel vapor in, increasing the charge in the cylinders. Superchargers are mechanically driven by the engine, using some of its power. Turbochargers do the same job but are driven by exhaust gases, so they don't use any of the engine's power. The power and efficiency of an engine can also be increased by fuel injectors, which have regulators that react to the engine's requirements by injecting exactly the right amount of fuel.

AIR AND GAS FLOW IN A TURBOCHARGER FOR A MODERN V6 ENGINE

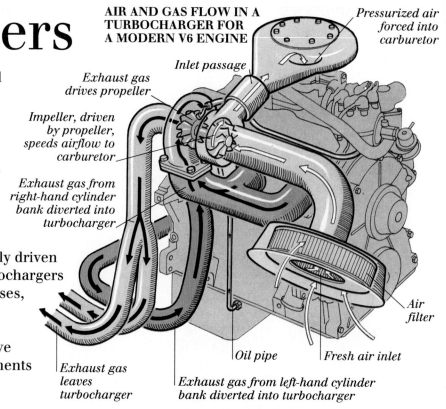

Pressurized air forced into carburetor

Inlet passage

Exhaust gas drives propeller

Impeller, driven by propeller, speeds airflow to carburetor

Exhaust gas from right-hand cylinder bank diverted into turbocharger

Air filter

Oil pipe

Fresh air inlet

Exhaust gas leaves turbocharger

Exhaust gas from left-hand cylinder bank diverted into turbocharger

PARTS OF A SUPERCHARGER, c.1948

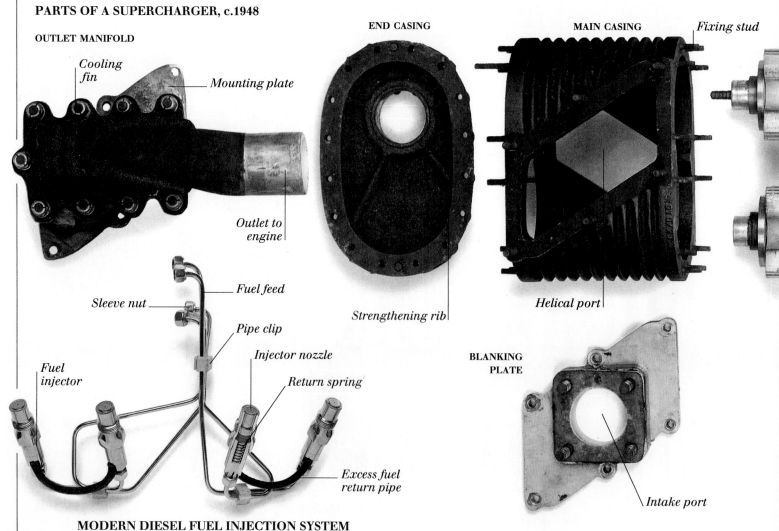

OUTLET MANIFOLD

Cooling fin

Mounting plate

Outlet to engine

END CASING

Strengthening rib

MAIN CASING

Fixing stud

Helical port

Fuel feed

Sleeve nut

Pipe clip

Injector nozzle

Fuel injector

Return spring

Excess fuel return pipe

BLANKING PLATE

Intake port

MODERN DIESEL FUEL INJECTION SYSTEM

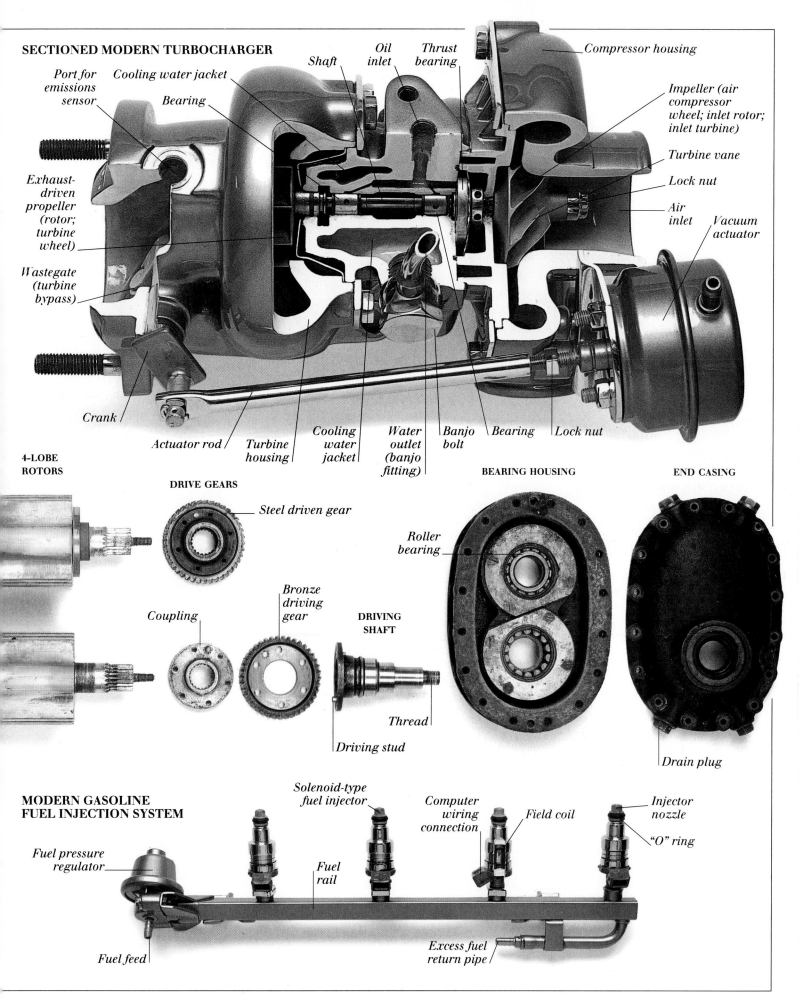

SECTIONED MODERN TURBOCHARGER

Port for emissions sensor

Cooling water jacket

Bearing

Shaft

Oil inlet

Thrust bearing

Compressor housing

Impeller (air compressor wheel; inlet rotor; inlet turbine)

Turbine vane

Lock nut

Air inlet

Vacuum actuator

Exhaust-driven propeller (rotor; turbine wheel)

Wastegate (turbine bypass)

Crank

Actuator rod

Turbine housing

Cooling water jacket

Water outlet (banjo fitting)

Banjo bolt

Bearing

Lock nut

4-LOBE ROTORS

DRIVE GEARS

Steel driven gear

Coupling

Bronze driving gear

DRIVING SHAFT

Thread

Driving stud

BEARING HOUSING

Roller bearing

END CASING

Drain plug

MODERN GASOLINE FUEL INJECTION SYSTEM

Solenoid-type fuel injector

Computer wiring connection

Field coil

Injector nozzle

"O" ring

Fuel pressure regulator

Fuel rail

Fuel feed

Excess fuel return pipe

Cooling and lubrication

COMBUSTION TEMPERATURES in an engine's cylinders can reach around 3,000°F (1,700°C), enough heat to melt the cylinder head. To prevent this, most cars have a water-cooling system, although a few cars use air-cooling. Coolant (water mixed with antifreeze) is circulated around a jacket surrounding the cylinders, then to a radiator, where the heat the coolant has absorbed is released into the air. Some heat may be used to warm the car's interior. Modern vehicles increasingly use separate air-conditioning systems to maintain a steady temperature. Oil lubrication also cools the engine, but its main role is to maintain a thin film of oil between moving parts to prevent wearing and seizing. Most lubrication systems circulate oil from a sump attached to the engine. The dry sump lubrication system, used in some competition cars, keeps oil in a separate tank to prevent the oil from overheating.

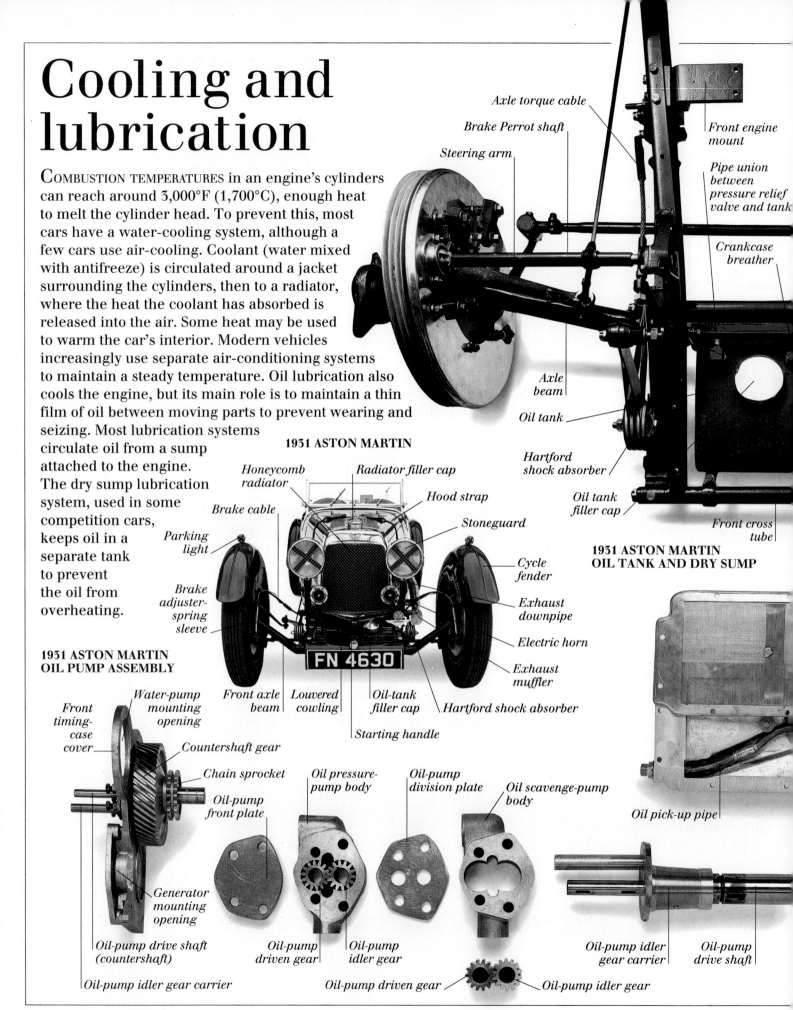

Axle torque cable

Brake Perrot shaft

Steering arm

Front engine mount

Pipe union between pressure relief valve and tank

Crankcase breather

Axle beam

Oil tank

Hartford shock absorber

Oil tank filler cap

Front cross tube

1931 ASTON MARTIN

Honeycomb radiator

Radiator filler cap

Hood strap

Brake cable

Stoneguard

Parking light

Cycle fender

Brake adjuster-spring sleeve

Exhaust downpipe

Electric horn

FN 4630

Exhaust muffler

Front axle beam

Louvered cowling

Oil-tank filler cap

Hartford shock absorber

Starting handle

1931 ASTON MARTIN OIL TANK AND DRY SUMP

1931 ASTON MARTIN OIL PUMP ASSEMBLY

Front timing-case cover

Water-pump mounting opening

Countershaft gear

Chain sprocket

Oil-pump front plate

Oil pressure-pump body

Oil-pump division plate

Oil scavenge-pump body

Generator mounting opening

Oil-pump drive shaft (countershaft)

Oil-pump driven gear

Oil-pump idler gear

Oil pick-up pipe

Oil-pump idler gear carrier

Oil-pump driven gear

Oil-pump idler gear

Oil-pump idler gear carrier

Oil-pump idler gear

Oil-pump drive shaft

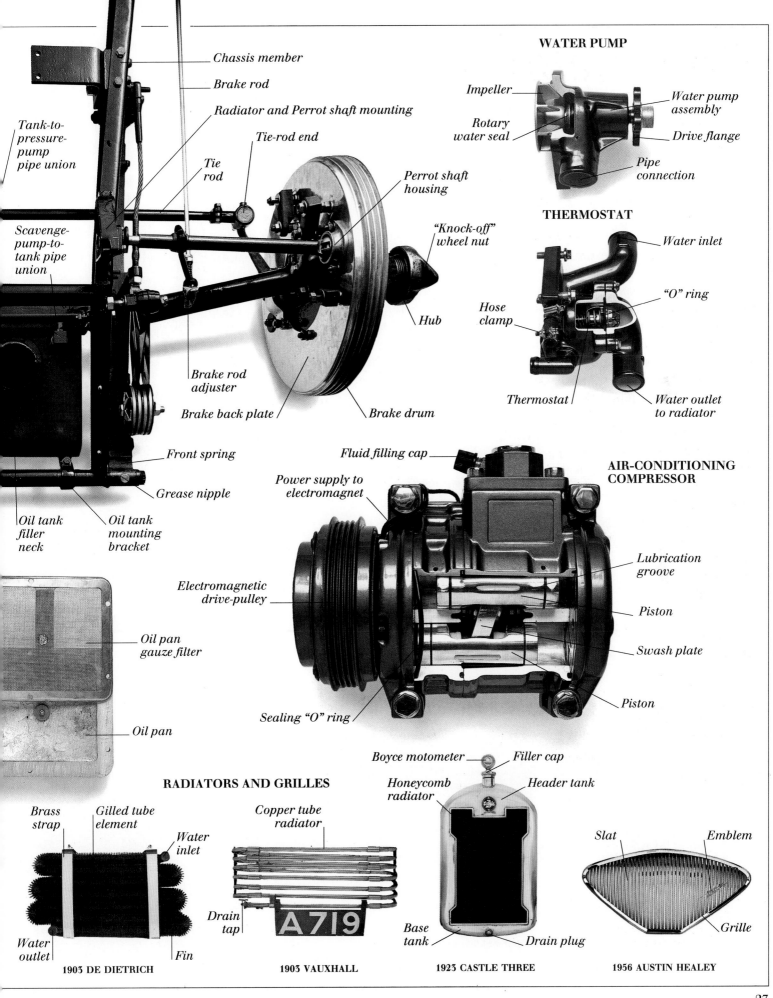

Chassis member

Brake rod

Radiator and Perrot shaft mounting

Tie-rod end

Tank-to-pressure-pump pipe union

Tie rod

Perrot shaft housing

WATER PUMP

Impeller

Water pump assembly

Rotary water seal

Drive flange

Pipe connection

Scavenge-pump-to-tank pipe union

"Knock-off" wheel nut

THERMOSTAT

Water inlet

Hose clamp

"O" ring

Hub

Water outlet to radiator

Thermostat

Brake rod adjuster

Brake back plate

Brake drum

Front spring

Grease nipple

Fluid filling cap

Power supply to electromagnet

AIR-CONDITIONING COMPRESSOR

Oil tank filler neck

Oil tank mounting bracket

Lubrication groove

Electromagnetic drive-pulley

Piston

Oil pan gauze filter

Swash plate

Piston

Oil pan

Sealing "O" ring

Boyce motometer

Filler cap

Honeycomb radiator

Header tank

RADIATORS AND GRILLES

Brass strap

Gilled tube element

Water inlet

Copper tube radiator

Slat

Emblem

Drain tap

Base tank

Drain plug

Grille

Water outlet

Fin

A719

1903 DE DIETRICH

1903 VAUXHALL

1923 CASTLE THREE

1956 AUSTIN HEALEY

Clutch and gearbox

THE GEARBOX TRANSMITS POWER from the engine to the road wheels. It also allows the wheels to turn at different speeds to the engine. Modern gearboxes contain five or six sets of intermeshed cogs (including a reverse gear set) to apply the turning force of the engine (torque) most efficiently over as wide a range of road speeds as possible and to enable the car to climb hills. To engage gears, or to remain stationary with the engine running, the engine must be disconnected from the gearbox. This is achieved by the clutch, which has one plate connected to the engine (the driving plate) and another connected to the gearbox (the driven plate). To disconnect the engine from the gearbox, the clutch plates are unclamped so that they are no longer in contact; for the engine to drive the wheels, strong springs clamp the plates together.

MODERN FRICTION CLUTCH ASSEMBLY

PRESSURE PLATE (DRIVING PLATE)
Leaf spring

DRIVEN PLATE
Rivet
Heat-resistant lining

FLYWHEEL
Crankshaft bolt hole

Gearbox spline (input shaft)
Starting motor ring gear
Clutch plate mounting hole

Clutch release rod

Feed for ignition burners
Dumb iron
Cross shaft
Starting handle
Gear selector linkage
Fuel tank
Dumb iron

Clutch bell-housing

MODERN 5-SPEED MANUAL GEARBOX

Countershaft band brake
Forward miter wheel (bevel gear)
Chain sprocket
Differential gear
Exhaust pipe
Steel and gunmetal spur wheel

Solid-tired artillery wheel

Reverse miter wheel (bevel gear)
Oil feed
Step
Iron subframe
Tiller
Drive shaft
Wooden car frame
Gear lever
Candle lamp

1895 PANHARD & LEVASSOR WITH CRASH GEARBOX

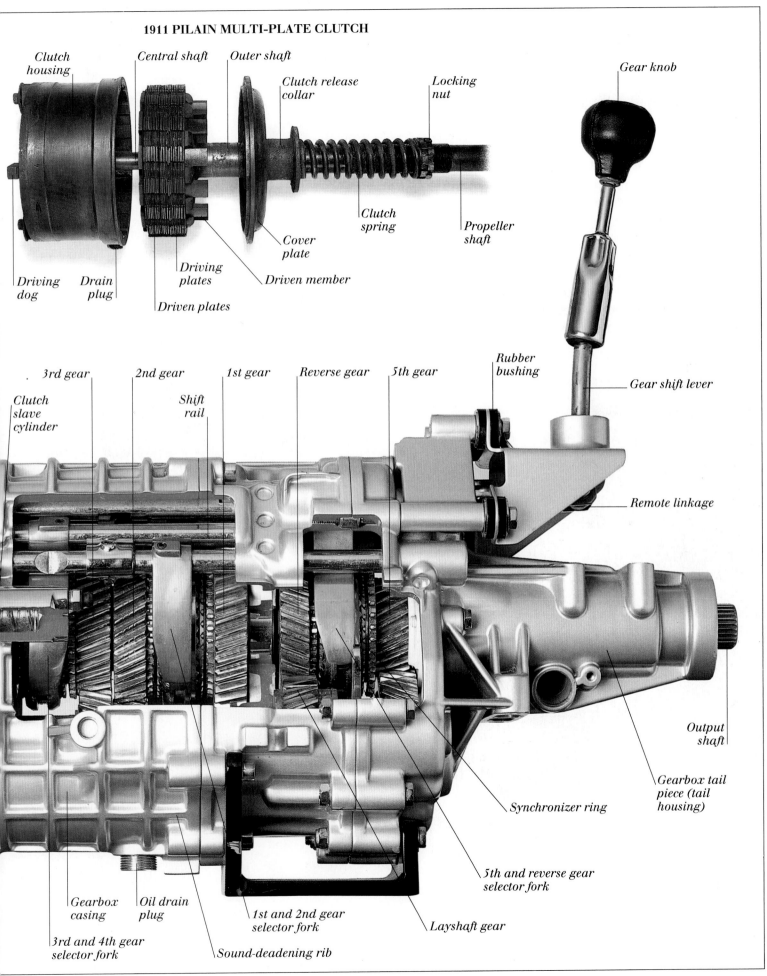

1911 PILAIN MULTI-PLATE CLUTCH

Clutch housing

Central shaft

Outer shaft

Clutch release collar

Locking nut

Gear knob

Driving dog

Drain plug

Driving plates

Driven plates

Cover plate

Driven member

Clutch spring

Propeller shaft

3rd gear

2nd gear

1st gear

Reverse gear

5th gear

Rubber bushing

Clutch slave cylinder

Shift rail

Gear shift lever

Remote linkage

Output shaft

Gearbox tail piece (tail housing)

Synchronizer ring

5th and reverse gear selector fork

Gearbox casing

Oil drain plug

1st and 2nd gear selector fork

Layshaft gear

3rd and 4th gear selector fork

Sound-deadening rib

Transmission systems

THE TRANSMISSION SYSTEM transmits the engine's power to the wheels. Early cars used chains or belts to achieve this. Modern cars use a clutch, gearbox, and drive shafts. Some modern cars have a continuously variable transmission, in which a belt runs between pulleys that expand and contract automatically to provide the right gearing ratio. The most common type of automatic gearbox contains planetary gear sets that are selected according to engine speed and throttle opening. Perhaps the most unusual form of transmission was that of the French Leyat, which had no clutch, gearbox, or final drive but was powered by a variable-speed propeller.

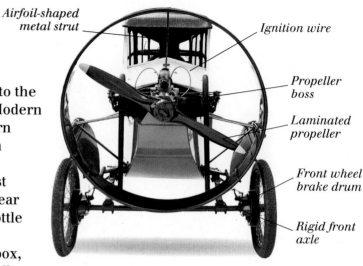

Airfoil-shaped metal strut

Ignition wire

Propeller boss

Laminated propeller

Front wheel brake drum

Rigid front axle

SIDE VIEW OF LEYAT

Fuselage

Rear fender

Steering cabane

Beaded edge tire

Propeller shield (airscrew shield)

Flat twin engine

Wire wheel

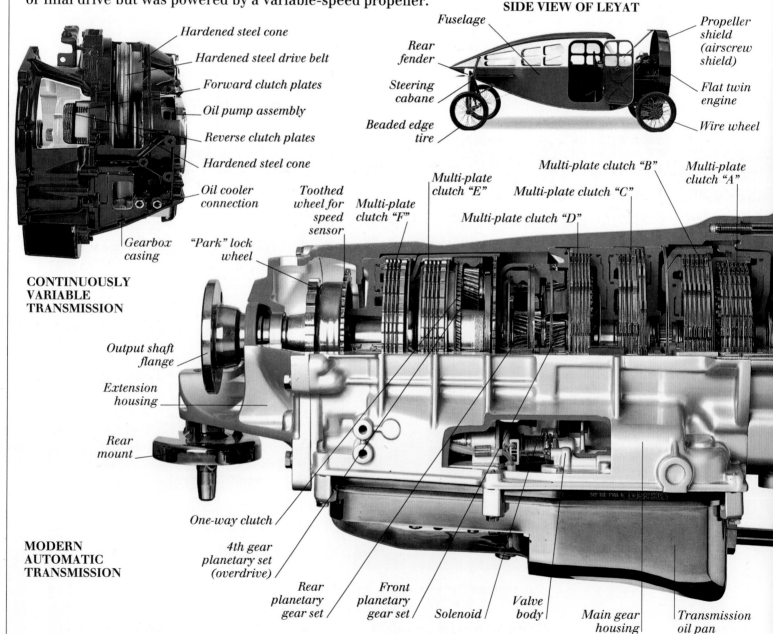

Hardened steel cone

Hardened steel drive belt

Forward clutch plates

Oil pump assembly

Reverse clutch plates

Hardened steel cone

Oil cooler connection

Gearbox casing

CONTINUOUSLY VARIABLE TRANSMISSION

"Park" lock wheel

Toothed wheel for speed sensor

Multi-plate clutch "F"

Multi-plate clutch "E"

Multi-plate clutch "D"

Multi-plate clutch "C"

Multi-plate clutch "B"

Multi-plate clutch "A"

Output shaft flange

Extension housing

Rear mount

MODERN AUTOMATIC TRANSMISSION

One-way clutch

4th gear planetary set (overdrive)

Rear planetary gear set

Front planetary gear set

Solenoid

Valve body

Main gear housing

Transmission oil pan

CHAIN-DRIVEN 70-HP MERCEDES, 1904

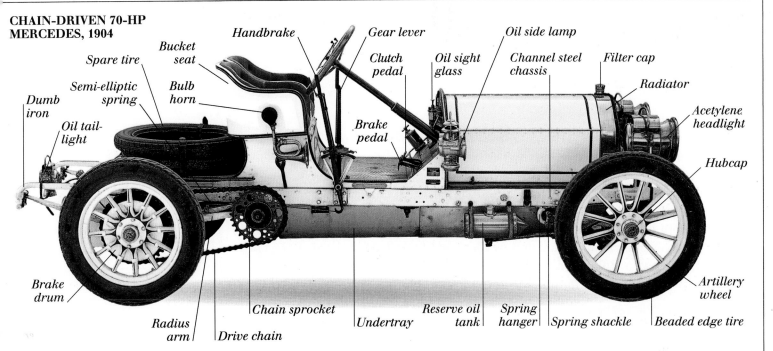

Spare tire

Bucket seat

Handbrake

Gear lever

Clutch pedal

Oil side lamp

Oil sight glass

Channel steel chassis

Filter cap

Radiator

Semi-elliptic spring

Bulb horn

Dumb iron

Oil tail-light

Brake pedal

Acetylene headlight

Hubcap

Brake drum

Radius arm

Drive chain

Chain sprocket

Undertray

Reserve oil tank

Spring hanger

Spring shackle

Beaded edge tire

Artillery wheel

BELT-DRIVEN DAIMLER MAYBACH, 1895

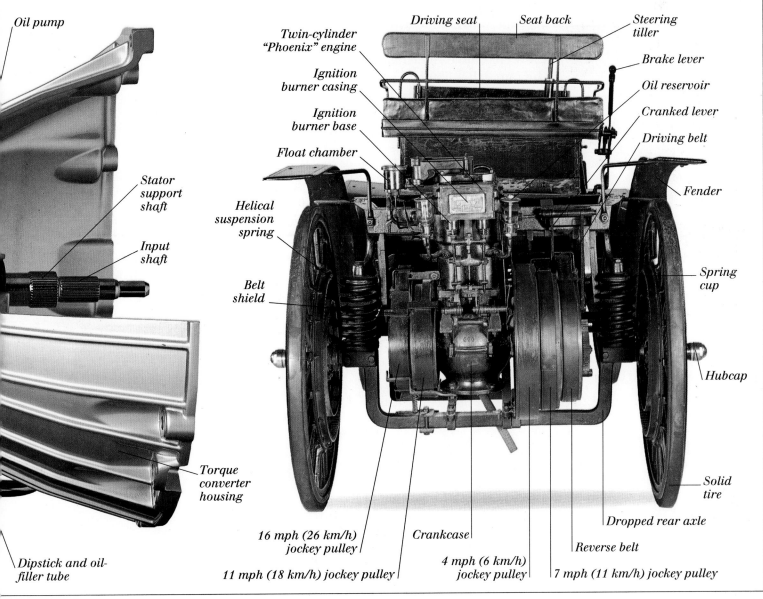

Oil pump

Driving seat

Seat back

Steering tiller

Twin-cylinder "Phoenix" engine

Brake lever

Oil reservoir

Ignition burner casing

Cranked lever

Ignition burner base

Driving belt

Float chamber

Fender

Stator support shaft

Input shaft

Helical suspension spring

Belt shield

Spring cup

Hubcap

Torque converter housing

Solid tire

Dipstick and oil-filler tube

16 mph (26 km/h) jockey pulley

11 mph (18 km/h) jockey pulley

Crankcase

4 mph (6 km/h) jockey pulley

Dropped rear axle

Reverse belt

7 mph (11 km/h) jockey pulley

Final drive and steering

Drive shaft

Gearbox

MOST EARLY CARS USED THE PANHARD transmission system, named after the manufacturer René Panhard, in which a front-mounted engine drove the rear wheels through a multiple-ratio gearbox. Since the late 1950s in Europe, and the early 1970s in the United States, most cars have used front-wheel drive. Today, powerful cars increasingly use four-wheel drive for its better road-holding. Whatever the drive system used, a driven axle is turned by a final-drive gear, usually located in the gearbox in front-wheel-drive cars. The final-drive gear incorporates a differential gear that allows the outer wheel to turn faster than the inner when driving around corners. In most cars, only the front wheels are steered. The steering column is joined by a pinion to a rack. When the steering wheel is turned, the pinion rolls the rack either right or left, so turning the wheels. Some cars have power-assisted steering, in which hydraulic power makes it easier for the driver to turn the steering wheel. A few cars have steering on all four wheels. The four-wheel-steering rack shown here an electronic control unit that controls the direction of the rear wheels, while the front wheels are steered conventionally.

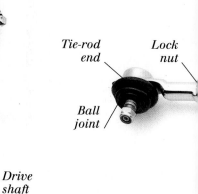

Tie-rod end

Lock nut

Ball joint

Tie rod

Dust cover

Drive shaft

FRONT VIEW OF A FOUR-WHEEL-DRIVE RENAULT ESPACE

FOUR-WHEEL-DRIVE RUNNING GEAR

Aerodynamic windshield

"Monobox" body

SIDE VIEW OF A FOUR-WHEEL-DRIVE RENAULT ESPACE

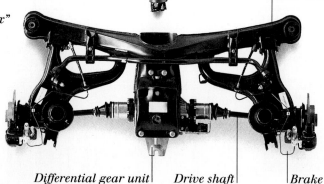

Rear axle

Differential gear unit   Drive shaft   Brake assembly

DIFFERENTIAL UNIT

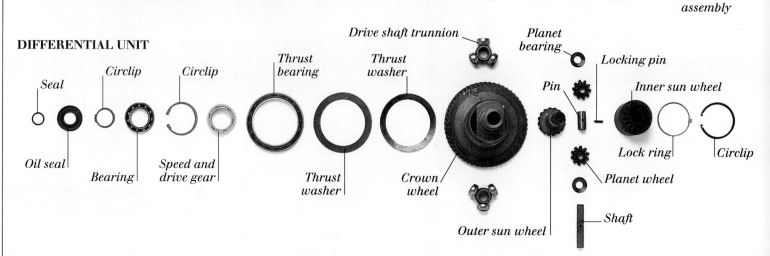

Seal

Circlip   Circlip

Drive shaft trunnion

Thrust bearing

Thrust washer

Planet bearing

Locking pin

Pin   Inner sun wheel

Oil seal

Bearing

Speed and drive gear

Thrust washer

Crown wheel

Lock ring   Circlip

Planet wheel

Shaft

Outer sun wheel

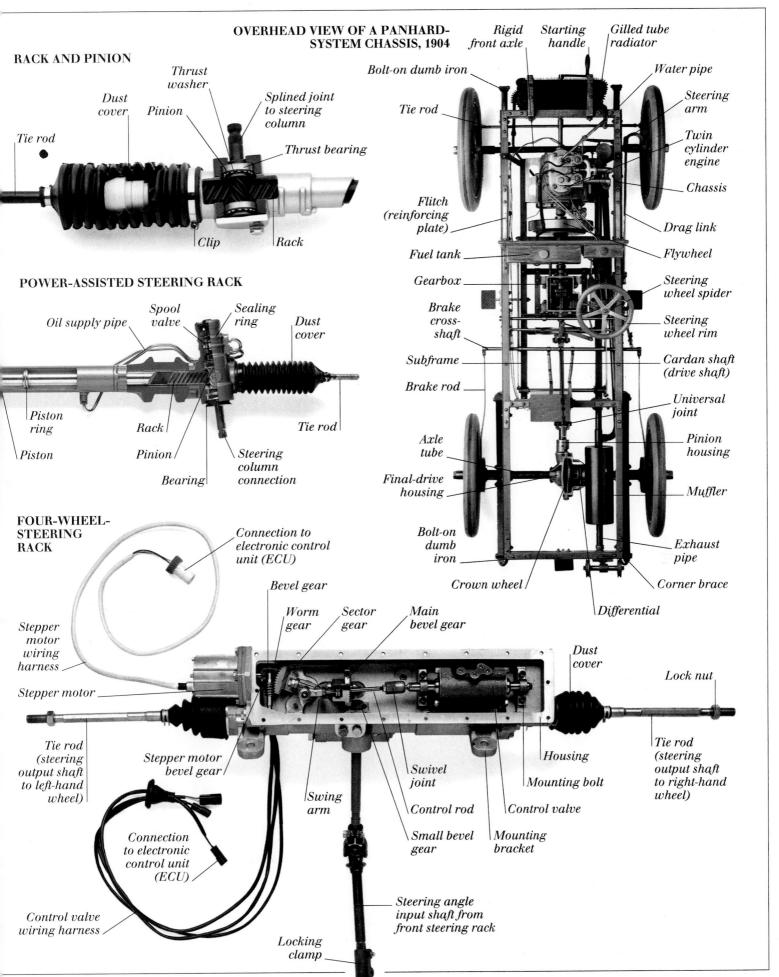

RACK AND PINION

Tie rod

Dust cover

Thrust washer

Pinion

Splined joint to steering column

Thrust bearing

Clip

Rack

POWER-ASSISTED STEERING RACK

Oil supply pipe

Spool valve

Sealing ring

Dust cover

Piston ring

Rack

Pinion

Bearing

Steering column connection

Tie rod

Piston

FOUR-WHEEL-STEERING RACK

Connection to electronic control unit (ECU)

Stepper motor wiring harness

Stepper motor

Tie rod (steering output shaft to left-hand wheel)

Stepper motor bevel gear

Connection to electronic control unit (ECU)

Control valve wiring harness

Swing arm

Locking clamp

Bevel gear

Worm gear

Sector gear

Main bevel gear

Small bevel gear

Control rod

Swivel joint

Control valve

Mounting bracket

Mounting bolt

Housing

Dust cover

Lock nut

Tie rod (steering output shaft to right-hand wheel)

Steering angle input shaft from front steering rack

OVERHEAD VIEW OF A PANHARD-SYSTEM CHASSIS, 1904

Rigid front axle

Starting handle

Gilled tube radiator

Bolt-on dumb iron

Water pipe

Tie rod

Steering arm

Twin cylinder engine

Chassis

Flitch (reinforcing plate)

Drag link

Fuel tank

Flywheel

Gearbox

Steering wheel spider

Brake cross-shaft

Steering wheel rim

Subframe

Cardan shaft (drive shaft)

Brake rod

Universal joint

Axle tube

Pinion housing

Final-drive housing

Muffler

Bolt-on dumb iron

Exhaust pipe

Crown wheel

Corner brace

Differential

33

Suspension

TWIN TRAILING ARM INDEPENDENT FRONT SUSPENSION

SUSPENSION CUSHIONS THE CAR from the effects of irregular road surfaces. It also helps to maintain maximum contact between the tires and the road, and so is necessary for effective steering, braking, and acceleration. The earliest suspension systems —leaf springs made of layers of steel leaves—are still used in some cars. Most modern cars use coil springs, which, unlike leaf springs, have no built-in damping to eliminate unwanted bouncing over rough surfaces. Coil springs require separate hydraulic or gas-filled shock absorbers to counteract this bouncing. The MacPherson strut is an independent system that combines shock absorbers and a king pin (which acts as a bearing for the steering movement) in one unit. The de Dion rear suspension system was invented a century ago, but is still used in some modern sports cars because it reduces wheel spin and gives better road-holding.

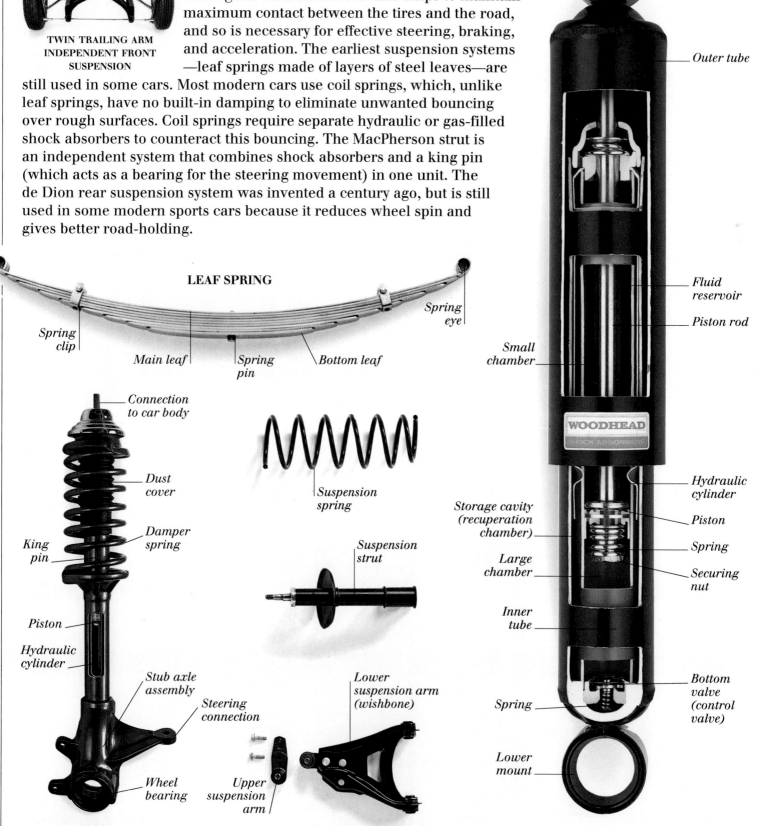

TELESCOPIC HYDRAULIC SHOCK ABSORBER, 1967

Chassis attachment eye (upper mount)

Outer tube

Fluid reservoir

Piston rod

Small chamber

Hydraulic cylinder

Storage cavity (recuperation chamber)

Piston

Large chamber

Spring

Securing nut

Inner tube

Spring

Bottom valve (control valve)

Lower mount

LEAF SPRING

Spring eye

Spring clip

Main leaf

Spring pin

Bottom leaf

Connection to car body

Dust cover

Damper spring

King pin

Suspension spring

Piston

Hydraulic cylinder

Suspension strut

Stub axle assembly

Steering connection

Wheel bearing

Upper suspension arm

Lower suspension arm (wishbone)

MACPHERSON STRUT

COIL AND WISHBONE SUSPENSION

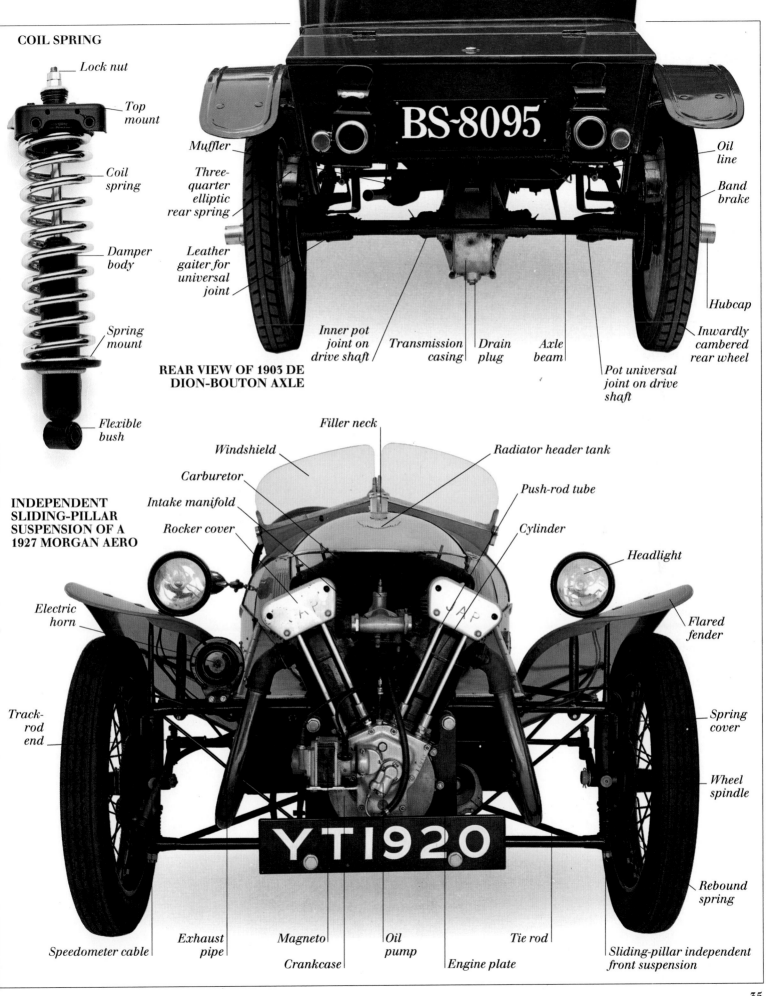

COIL SPRING

Lock nut

Top mount

Coil spring

Damper body

Spring mount

Flexible bush

REAR VIEW OF 1903 DE DION-BOUTON AXLE

Muffler

Three-quarter elliptic rear spring

Leather gaiter for universal joint

Inner pot joint on drive shaft

Transmission casing

Drain plug

Axle beam

Pot universal joint on drive shaft

Oil line

Band brake

Hubcap

Inwardly cambered rear wheel

BS-8095

INDEPENDENT SLIDING-PILLAR SUSPENSION OF A 1927 MORGAN AERO

Filler neck

Windshield

Carburetor

Intake manifold

Rocker cover

Radiator header tank

Push-rod tube

Cylinder

Headlight

Electric horn

Flared fender

Track-rod end

Spring cover

Wheel spindle

Rebound spring

Speedometer cable

Exhaust pipe

Magneto

Crankcase

Oil pump

Engine plate

Tie rod

Sliding-pillar independent front suspension

YT1920

Wheels and tires

IT IS NOT ENOUGH FOR A CAR WHEEL SIMPLY TO BE ROUND; it must also be strong enough to withstand violent stresses and carefully balanced so that it rotates evenly. It must be light yet stiff so that it does not affect the steering and suspension, and must allow air to flow over and cool the brakes. Early cars had wooden-spoked wheels, as did horse-drawn carriages, but such wheels can be distorted by heavy loads and by shrinkage. Wire wheels, derived from bicycle wheels, effectively hang the car from the wheel rim by precisely-tensioned thin spokes. The simplest form of modern wheel is the pressed steel disc, while cast aluminium wheels permit wider (low-profile) tires to be fitted for better grip (see pp. 46-47). The first tires were made from solid rubber but they were superseded by pneumatic (air-filled) tires, which provided a more comfortable ride. A major advance came with the introduction of radial-ply tires in the 1950s—their flexible sidewalls give better cornering and longer tread life.

"BIBENDUM," TRADEMARK OF THE MICHELIN TIRE COMPANY

HUB

Bolt-on plate

Spoke hole

Splines / Thread

"Knock-off" nut

Dowel

Rounded tongue to enter felloe

Belly

ARTILLERY WHEEL (WOODEN-SPOKED WHEEL)

Spoke

Felloe

Bolt hole for hub

Ring of felloes

Face of spoke

Knock

Hole for spoke

MICHELIN

TYPES OF TIRE

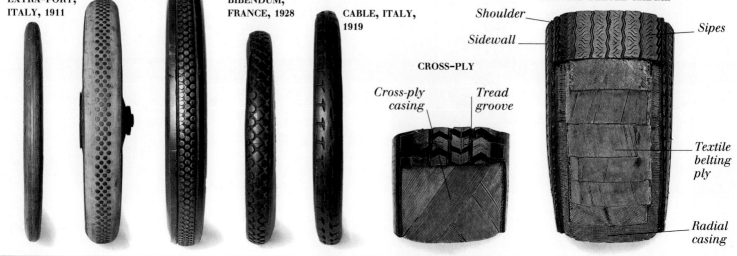

METAL-STUDDED NON-SKID, ITALY, 1914

RUBBER-STUDDED, FRANCE, 1926

EXTRA-FORT, ITALY, 1911

CONFORT BIBENDUM, FRANCE, 1928

CABLE, ITALY, 1919

TEXTILE-BELTED RADIAL

Shoulder

Sidewall

Sipes

CROSS-PLY

Cross-ply casing

Tread groove

Textile belting ply

Radial casing

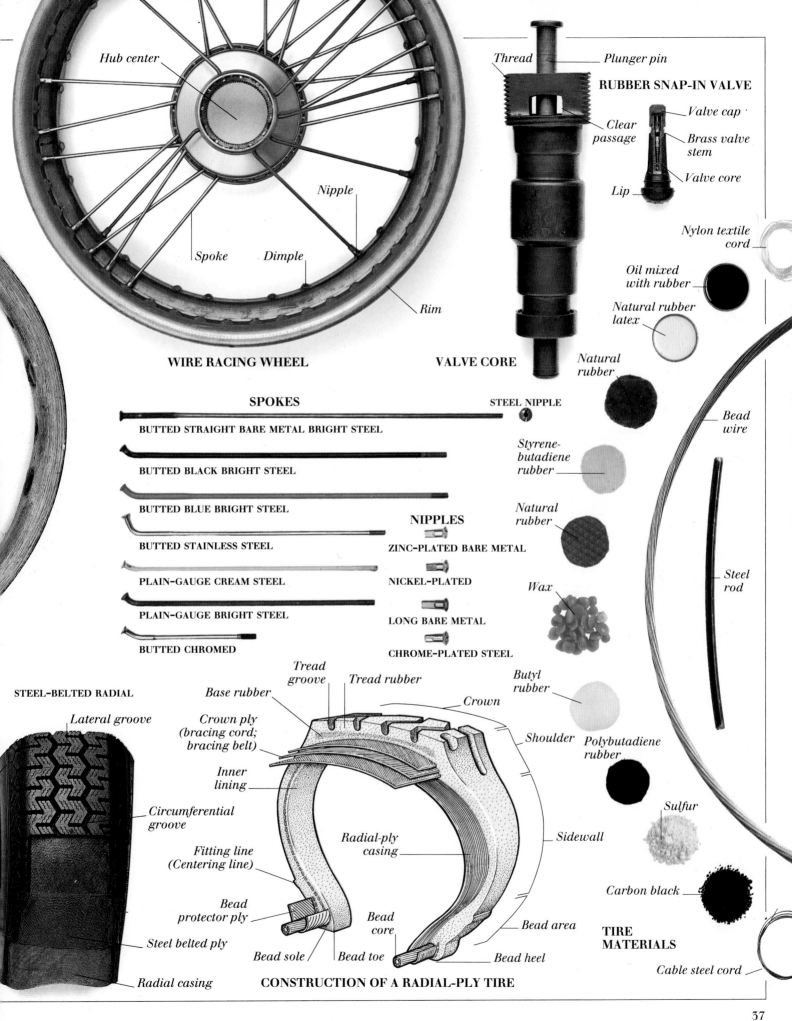

Hub center

Nipple

Spoke **Dimple**

Rim

WIRE RACING WHEEL

Thread **Plunger pin**

RUBBER SNAP-IN VALVE

Clear passage

Valve cap

Brass valve stem

Valve core

Lip

VALVE CORE

SPOKES **STEEL NIPPLE**

BUTTED STRAIGHT BARE METAL BRIGHT STEEL

BUTTED BLACK BRIGHT STEEL

BUTTED BLUE BRIGHT STEEL

BUTTED STAINLESS STEEL

NIPPLES

PLAIN–GAUGE CREAM STEEL

PLAIN–GAUGE BRIGHT STEEL

BUTTED CHROMED

ZINC–PLATED BARE METAL

NICKEL–PLATED

LONG BARE METAL

CHROME–PLATED STEEL

Nylon textile cord

Oil mixed with rubber

Natural rubber latex

Natural rubber

Styrene-butadiene rubber

Natural rubber

Wax

Bead wire

Steel rod

Butyl rubber

Polybutadiene rubber

STEEL–BELTED RADIAL

Lateral groove

Circumferential groove

Tread groove

Base rubber

Crown ply (bracing cord; bracing belt)

Inner lining

Fitting line (Centering line)

Bead protector ply

Steel belted ply

Radial casing

Tread rubber

Crown

Shoulder

Radial-ply casing

Sidewall

Bead area

Bead sole *Bead toe*

Bead core

Bead heel

CONSTRUCTION OF A RADIAL-PLY TIRE

Sulfur

Carbon black

TIRE MATERIALS

Cable steel cord

Brakes

BRAKES WERE A WEAK POINT of early cars. They often exerted uneven pressure on the wheels, causing the vehicle to pull to one side. Many early cars had wraparound band brakes, but they performed poorly when wet. Drum brakes (brake shoes that expand internally in a drum) on all four wheels became standard in the 1920s, but when used repeatedly, such brakes "fade" (when heat distorts the drums), leading to temporary loss of braking power. The solution, discovered in the 1950s, was to use disc brakes, in which brake pads press against a heat-conducting metal disc. Now, cars use drum brakes only on the rear wheels and disc brakes on the front or on all four wheels.

MODERN DRUM BRAKE

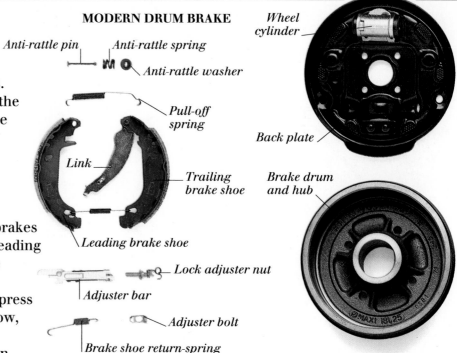

Anti-rattle pin
Anti-rattle spring
Anti-rattle washer
Pull-off spring
Link
Trailing brake shoe
Leading brake shoe
Lock adjuster nut
Adjuster bar
Adjuster bolt
Brake shoe return-spring
Wheel cylinder
Back plate
Brake drum and hub

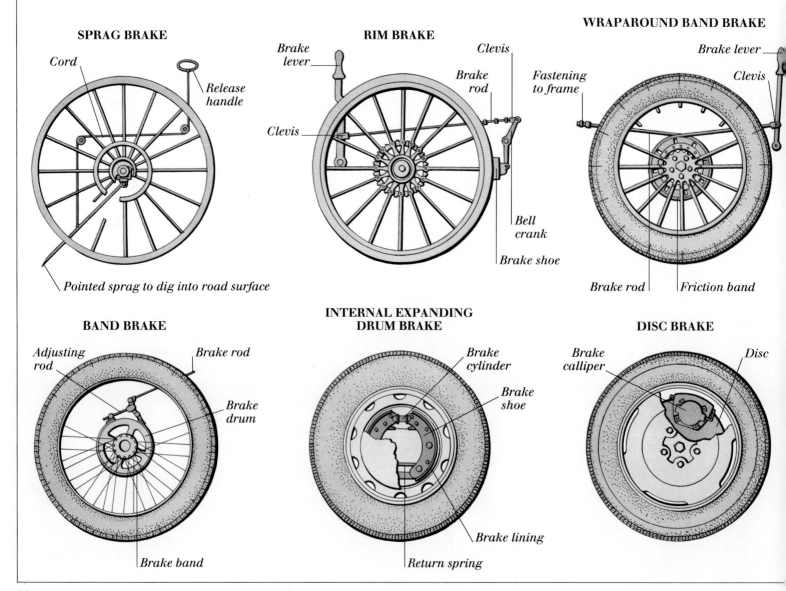

SPRAG BRAKE
Cord
Release handle
Pointed sprag to dig into road surface

RIM BRAKE
Brake lever
Clevis
Brake rod
Fastening to frame
Clevis
Bell crank
Brake shoe

WRAPAROUND BAND BRAKE
Brake lever
Clevis
Brake rod
Friction band

BAND BRAKE
Adjusting rod
Brake rod
Brake drum
Brake band

INTERNAL EXPANDING DRUM BRAKE
Brake cylinder
Brake shoe
Brake lining
Return spring

DISC BRAKE
Brake calliper
Disc

MODERN FRONT WHEEL DISC BRAKE

FRONT AND REAR VIEWS OF ANTILOCK BRAKING SYSTEM

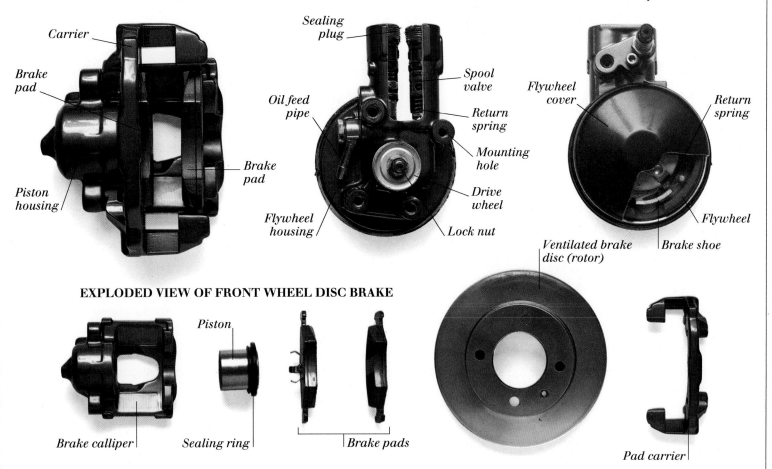

Carrier

Brake pad

Piston housing

Brake pad

Sealing plug

Oil feed pipe

Spool valve

Return spring

Mounting hole

Drive wheel

Flywheel housing

Lock nut

Flywheel cover

Return spring

Flywheel

Brake shoe

Ventilated brake disc (rotor)

EXPLODED VIEW OF FRONT WHEEL DISC BRAKE

Piston

Brake calliper

Sealing ring

Brake pads

Pad carrier

MARKUS MOTOR CARRIAGE WITH WOODEN BLOCK BRAKES, 1887

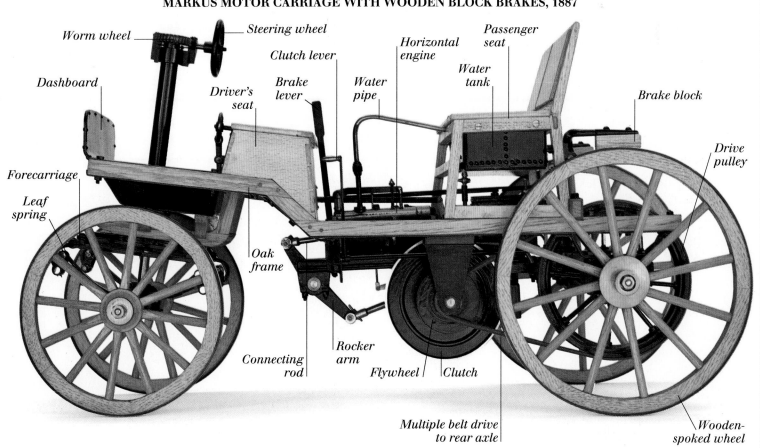

Worm wheel

Steering wheel

Dashboard

Clutch lever

Horizontal engine

Passenger seat

Driver's seat

Brake lever

Water pipe

Water tank

Brake block

Forecarriage

Leaf spring

Oak frame

Drive pulley

Connecting rod

Rocker arm

Flywheel

Clutch

Multiple belt drive to rear axle

Wooden-spoked wheel

Instruments

THE FIRST CARS REQUIRED such frequent attention to fuel, water, and lubricants that no instruments were necessary. The 1904 Mercedes (below) has a "brake-and-gradient meter" for indicating the efficiency of the car, but no speedometer. As the performance of cars improved, speed indicators, like the Cowey and Bowden meters shown here, appeared. The Cowey could also record the speed traveled at points 50 yards apart over the previous 750 yards. Soon, simple fuel and water gauges were added. Modern instrument panels monitor performance using electronic rather than mechanical means. Their readouts are often digital, as shown at right.

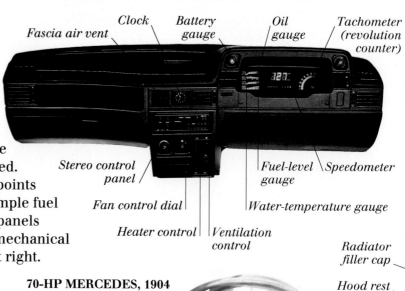

MODERN DIGITAL INSTRUMENT PANEL

Fascia air vent
Clock
Battery gauge
Oil gauge
Tachometer (revolution counter)
Stereo control panel
Fan control dial
Heater control
Ventilation control
Fuel-level gauge
Speedometer
Water-temperature gauge

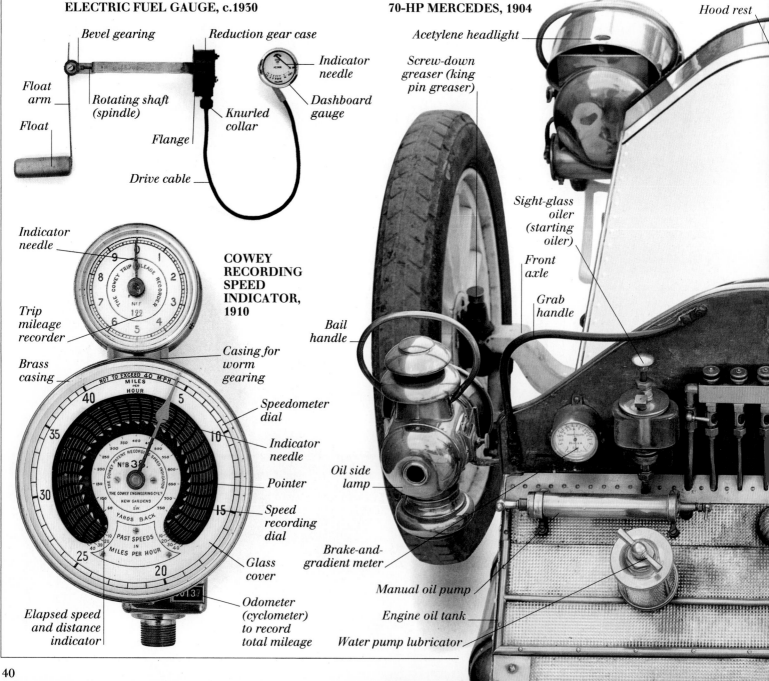

ELECTRIC FUEL GAUGE, c.1930

Bevel gearing
Reduction gear case
Float arm
Rotating shaft (spindle)
Float
Flange
Knurled collar
Drive cable
Indicator needle
Dashboard gauge

COWEY RECORDING SPEED INDICATOR, 1910

Indicator needle
Trip mileage recorder
Brass casing
Casing for worm gearing
Speedometer dial
Indicator needle
Pointer
Speed recording dial
Glass cover
Bail handle
Elapsed speed and distance indicator
Odometer (cyclometer) to record total mileage

NOT TO EXCEED 40 M.P.H
MILES PER HOUR
YARDS BACK
PAST SPEEDS IN MILES PER HOUR

70-HP MERCEDES, 1904

Acetylene headlight
Screw-down greaser (king pin greaser)
Radiator filler cap
Hood rest
Sight-glass oiler (starting oiler)
Front axle
Grab handle
Oil side lamp
Brake-and-gradient meter
Manual oil pump
Engine oil tank
Water pump lubricator

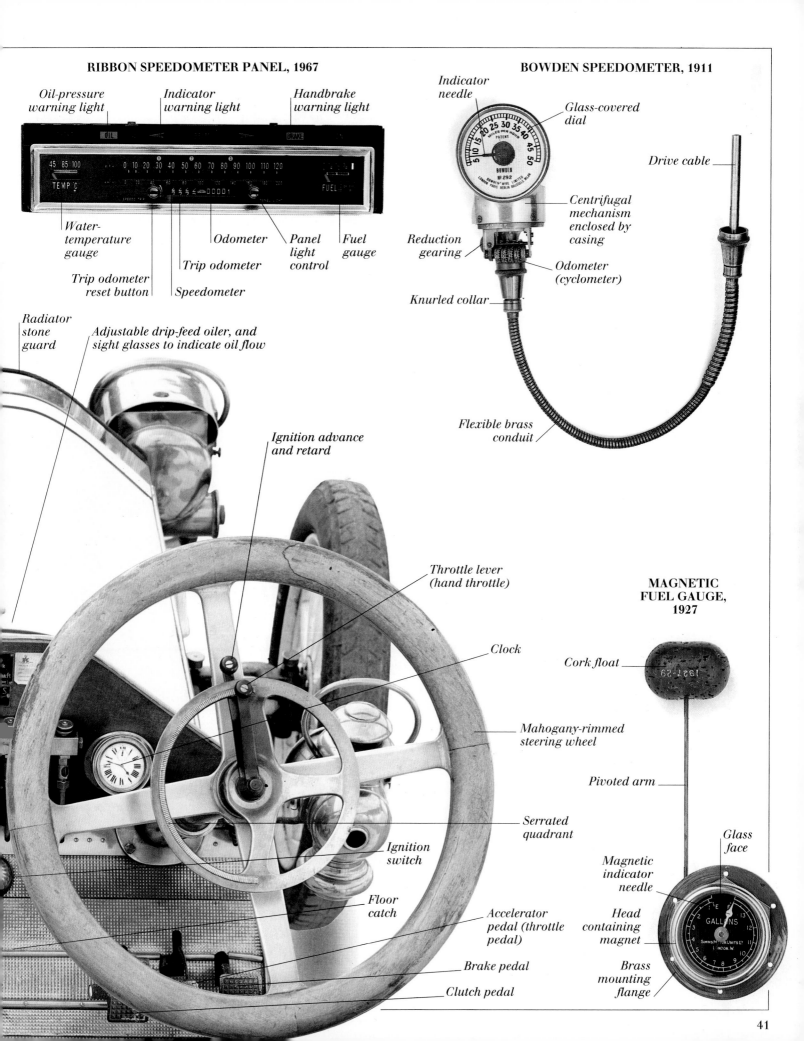

RIBBON SPEEDOMETER PANEL, 1967

Oil-pressure warning light

Indicator warning light

Handbrake warning light

Water-temperature gauge

Trip odometer reset button

Trip odometer

Speedometer

Odometer

Panel light control

Fuel gauge

BOWDEN SPEEDOMETER, 1911

Indicator needle

Glass-covered dial

Drive cable

Centrifugal mechanism enclosed by casing

Reduction gearing

Odometer (cyclometer)

Knurled collar

Flexible brass conduit

Radiator stone guard

Adjustable drip-feed oiler, and sight glasses to indicate oil flow

Ignition advance and retard

Throttle lever (hand throttle)

Clock

Mahogany-rimmed steering wheel

Serrated quadrant

Ignition switch

Floor catch

Accelerator pedal (throttle pedal)

Brake pedal

Clutch pedal

MAGNETIC FUEL GAUGE, 1927

Cork float

Pivoted arm

Glass face

Magnetic indicator needle

Head containing magnet

Brass mounting flange

Electrical systems

THE FIRST USE OF ELECTRICITY in cars was small batteries used to power the ignition system. The first electric headlamps appeared in 1905 and gradually replaced those using acetylene gas. Electricity is used extensively in modern cars. Lighting, ignition, locking, windows, stereo systems, instruments, and alarms are all controlled electrically, and are linked to the power source by a complex wiring harness (loom). Today, electrical systems often incorporate computers, which may control various functions, even including adjusting the position of the driver's seat to suit the needs of individual drivers.

MERCEDES COMPUTERIZED ELECTRIC SEAT

Drive belt

Back release

Backrest release

Seat belt

Drive cable

Head restraint motor

Back-lock motor

Runner

Gearbox

Gearbox and backrest adjustment motor

Fire extinguisher mounting bracket

Front seat lift

Main control harness

DRIP-FEED ACETYLENE GENERATOR, 1911

Lid for carbide chamber

Retaining nut

Carbide chamber

Water chamber

WIRING HARNESS OF A MODERN CAR

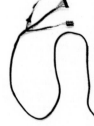

Left-hand taillight

Rear lights harness

License plate light

Right-hand taillight

Rear windshield heater and trunk light harness

Rear wiper harness

Left-hand rear shelf speaker

Right-hand rear shelf speaker

Radio antenna

Door radio speaker

Fuse board assembly

Fuse box

Lighting switch

Dash harness

Instrument panel assembly

Wiper switch

Right-hand side harness

EXAMPLES OF HEADLIGHTS

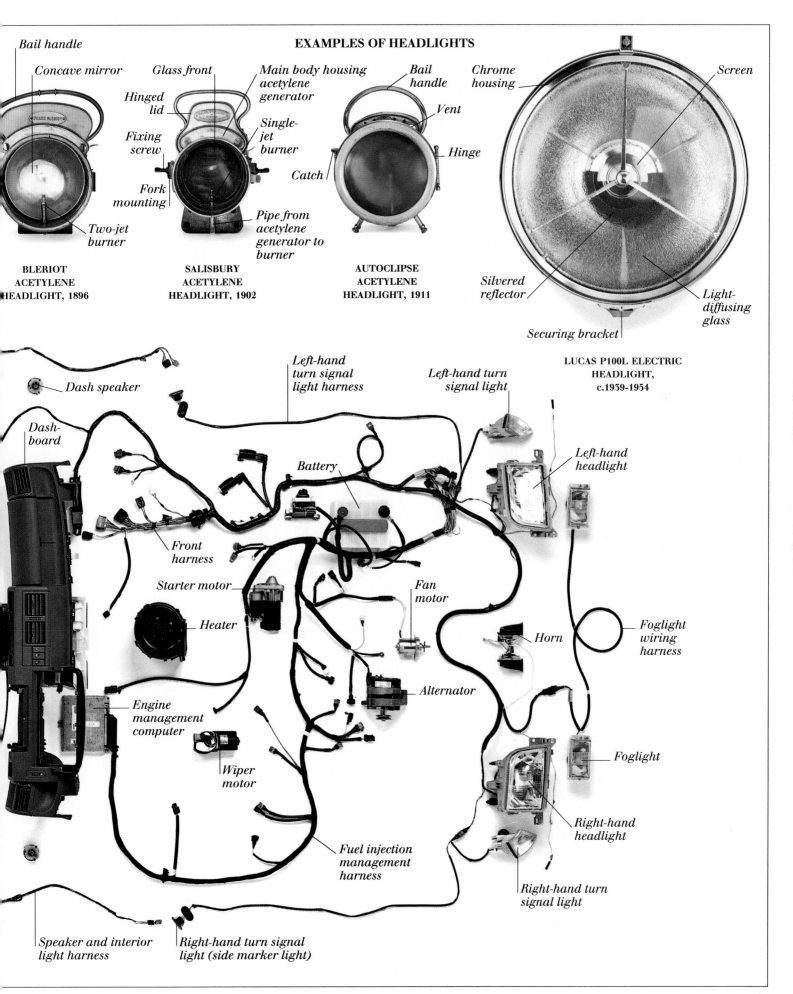

Bail handle

Concave mirror

Two-jet burner

BLERIOT ACETYLENE HEADLIGHT, 1896

Glass front

Hinged lid

Fixing screw

Fork mounting

Main body housing acetylene generator

Single-jet burner

Pipe from acetylene generator to burner

SALISBURY ACETYLENE HEADLIGHT, 1902

Bail handle

Vent

Hinge

Catch

AUTOCLIPSE ACETYLENE HEADLIGHT, 1911

Chrome housing

Screen

Silvered reflector

Securing bracket

Light-diffusing glass

LUCAS P100L ELECTRIC HEADLIGHT, c.1939-1954

Dash speaker

Dash-board

Left-hand turn signal light harness

Left-hand turn signal light

Battery

Left-hand headlight

Front harness

Starter motor

Heater

Fan motor

Horn

Foglight wiring harness

Alternator

Engine management computer

Wiper motor

Foglight

Right-hand headlight

Fuel injection management harness

Right-hand turn signal light

Speaker and interior light harness

Right-hand turn signal light (side marker light)

Modern bodywork

THE BODY OF A MODERN MASS-PRODUCED CAR is built on the monocoque (single-shell) principle, in which the roof, side panels, and floor are welded into a single integral unit. This bodyshell protects and supports the car's internal parts. Steel and glass are used to construct the bodyshell, creating a unit that is both light and strong. Its lightness helps to conserve energy, while its strength protects the occupants. Modern bodywork is designed with the aid of computers, which are used to predict factors such as aerodynamic efficiency and impact resistance. High technology is also employed on the production line, where robots are used to assemble, weld, and paint the body.

RENAULT LOGO

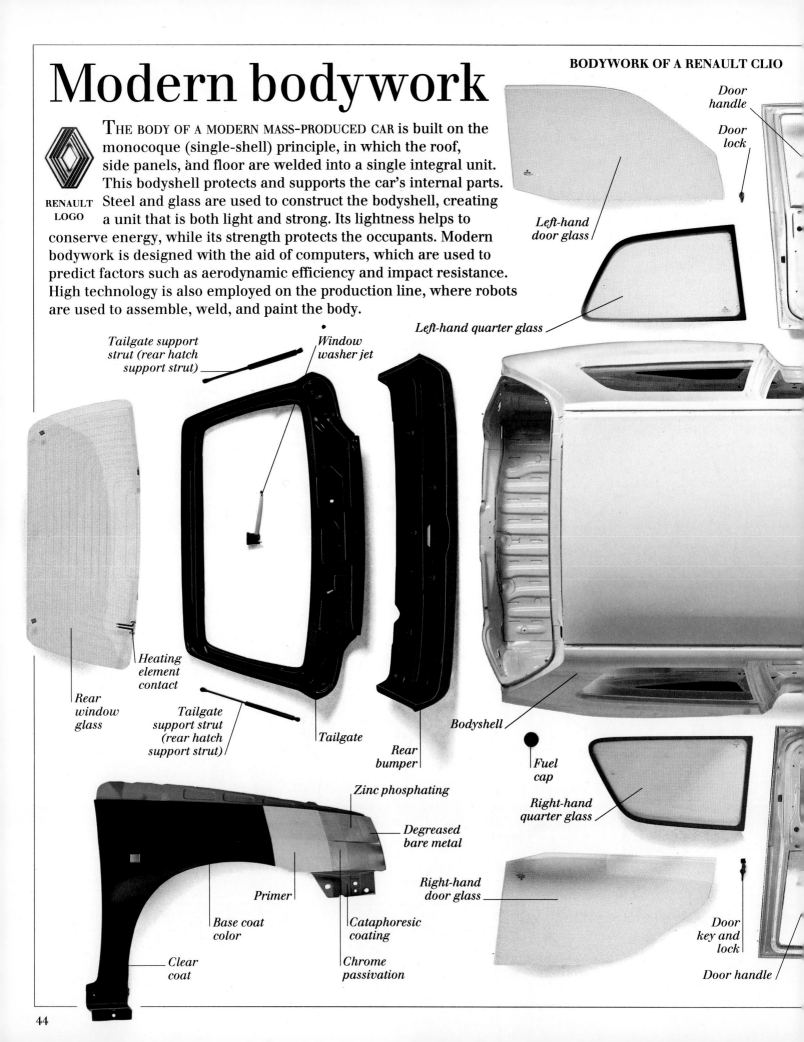

Door handle

Door lock

Left-hand door glass

Left-hand quarter glass

Tailgate support strut (rear hatch support strut)

Window washer jet

Rear window glass

Heating element contact

Tailgate support strut (rear hatch support strut)

Tailgate

Rear bumper

Bodyshell

Fuel cap

Right-hand quarter glass

Zinc phosphating

Degreased bare metal

Primer

Base coat color

Cataphoresic coating

Right-hand door glass

Clear coat

Chrome passivation

Door key and lock

Door handle

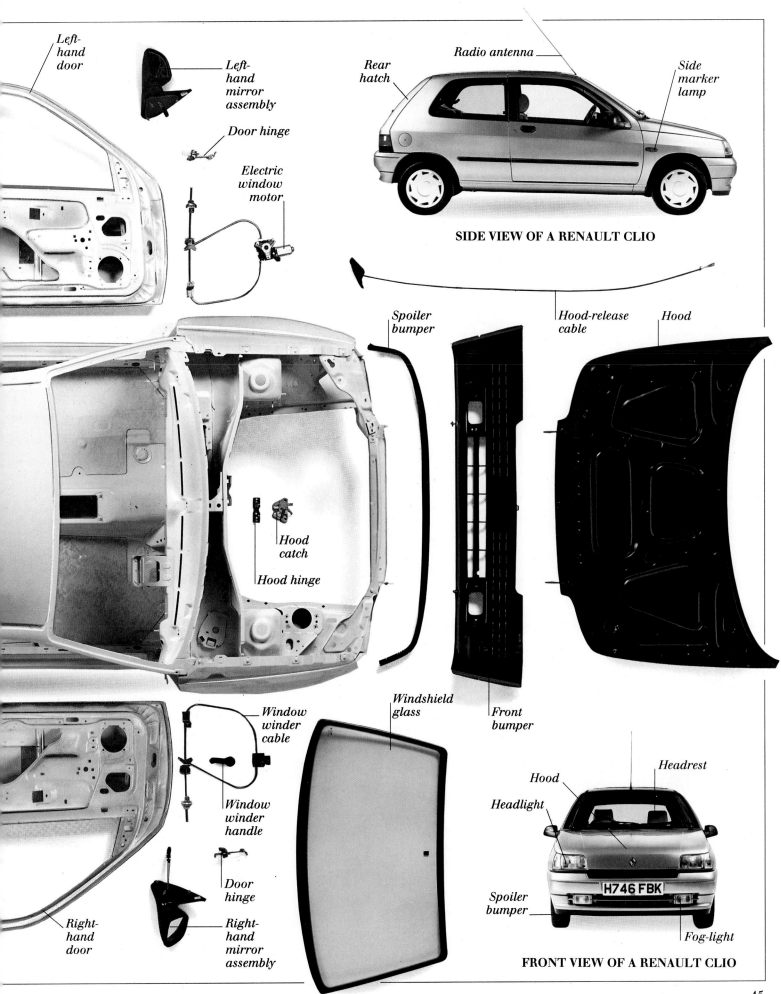

Left-hand door

Left-hand mirror assembly

Door hinge

Electric window motor

Radio antenna

Rear hatch

Side marker lamp

SIDE VIEW OF A RENAULT CLIO

Spoiler bumper

Hood-release cable

Hood

Hood catch

Hood hinge

Front bumper

Window winder cable

Windshield glass

Window winder handle

Door hinge

Right-hand door

Right-hand mirror assembly

Hood

Headrest

Headlight

Spoiler bumper

Fog-light

H746 FBK

FRONT VIEW OF A RENAULT CLIO

Modern components

A TYPICAL MODERN CAR has several thousand individual mechanical components. These are assembled to form the car's various mechanical systems: engine and exhaust, transmission, steering, suspension, and brakes. To ensure that each system functions properly, components are manufactured to extremely fine tolerances—to within about one ten-thousandth of an inch in some cases.

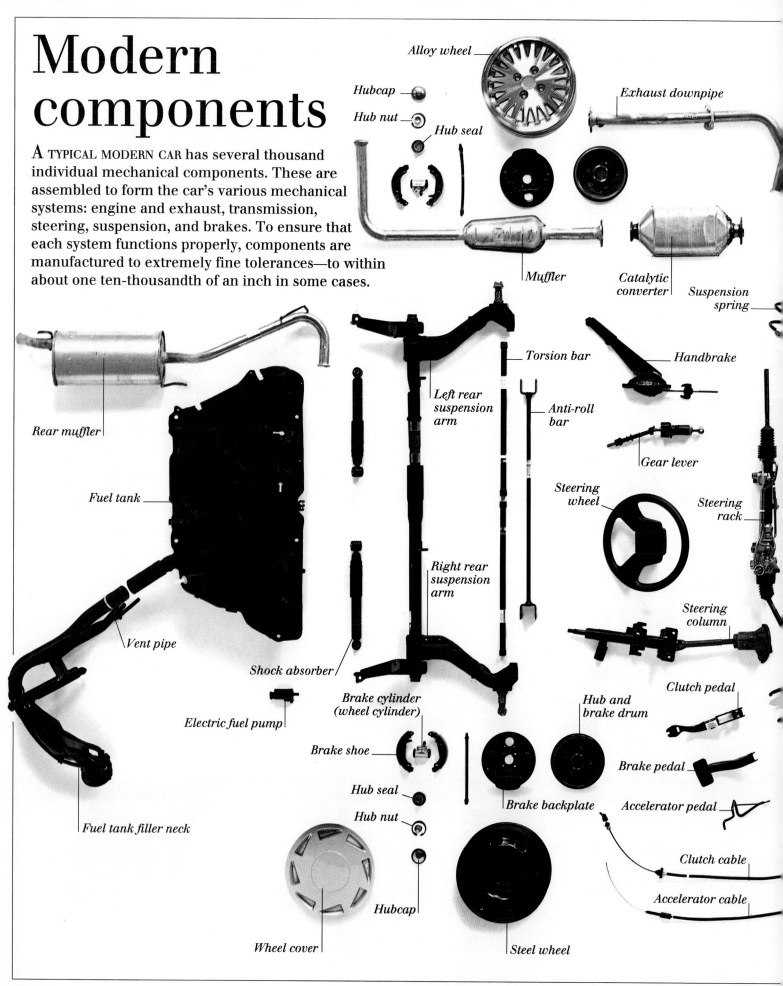

Alloy wheel

Hubcap

Hub nut

Hub seal

Exhaust downpipe

Muffler

Catalytic converter

Suspension spring

Rear muffler

Fuel tank

Vent pipe

Shock absorber

Electric fuel pump

Fuel tank filler neck

Torsion bar

Left rear suspension arm

Anti-roll bar

Right rear suspension arm

Handbrake

Gear lever

Steering wheel

Steering rack

Steering column

Clutch pedal

Hub and brake drum

Brake cylinder (wheel cylinder)

Brake shoe

Hub seal

Hub nut

Brake backplate

Brake pedal

Accelerator pedal

Clutch cable

Accelerator cable

Wheel cover

Hubcap

Steel wheel

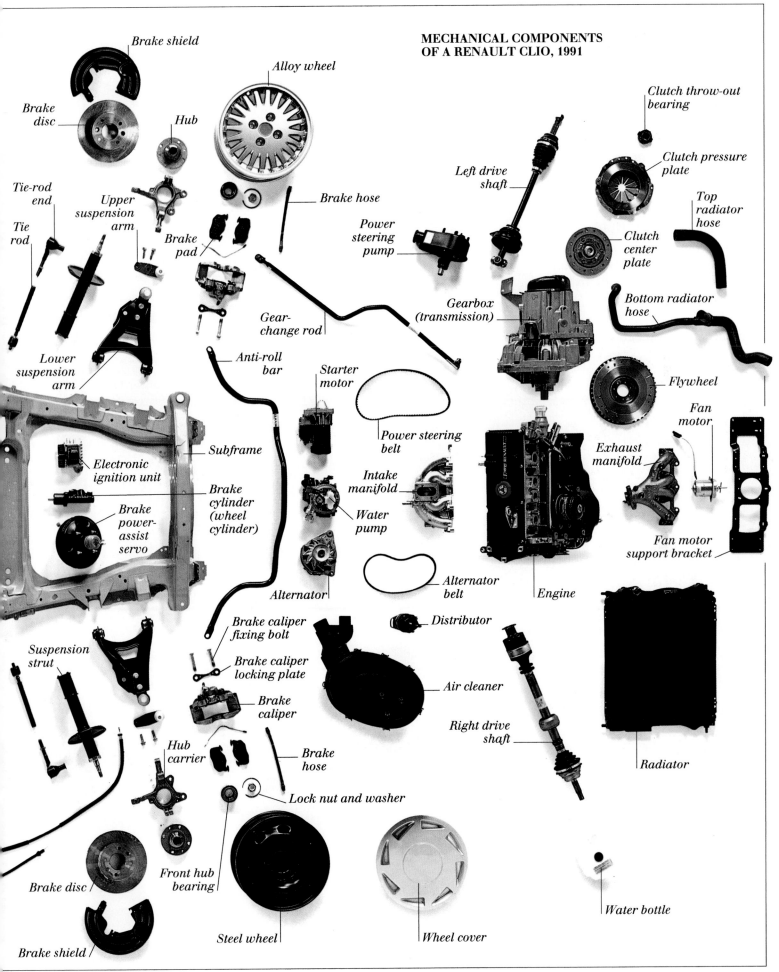

Brake shield

Brake disc

Hub

Alloy wheel

Brake hose

Clutch throw-out bearing

Left drive shaft

Clutch pressure plate

Tie-rod end

Upper suspension arm

Brake pad

Power steering pump

Top radiator hose

Tie rod

Clutch center plate

Bottom radiator hose

Gear-change rod

Gearbox (transmission)

Lower suspension arm

Anti-roll bar

Starter motor

Flywheel

Electronic ignition unit

Subframe

Power steering belt

Fan motor

Exhaust manifold

Brake cylinder (wheel cylinder)

Intake manifold

Brake power-assist servo

Water pump

Fan motor support bracket

Alternator belt

Alternator

Engine

Brake caliper fixing bolt

Distributor

Suspension strut

Brake caliper locking plate

Air cleaner

Brake caliper

Right drive shaft

Hub carrier

Brake hose

Radiator

Lock nut and washer

Brake disc

Front hub bearing

Steel wheel

Wheel cover

Water bottle

Brake shield

47

Modern trim

A MODERN CAR HAS TWO TYPES OF TRIM, according to the materials used: hard (chrome and plastics) and soft (upholstered materials). Safety and comfort are priorities in the trim's design: seats help the occupants to maintain a comfortable posture, rubber seals keep out dirt and moisture, and headlights light the way. Older cars had interior or leather paneling cut and fitted by craftsmen; modern cars use precisely molded plastics and seat fabrics cut by robot-controlled lasers to reduce costs and production time. Doors are now assembled off the production line so that complex wiring can be built in.

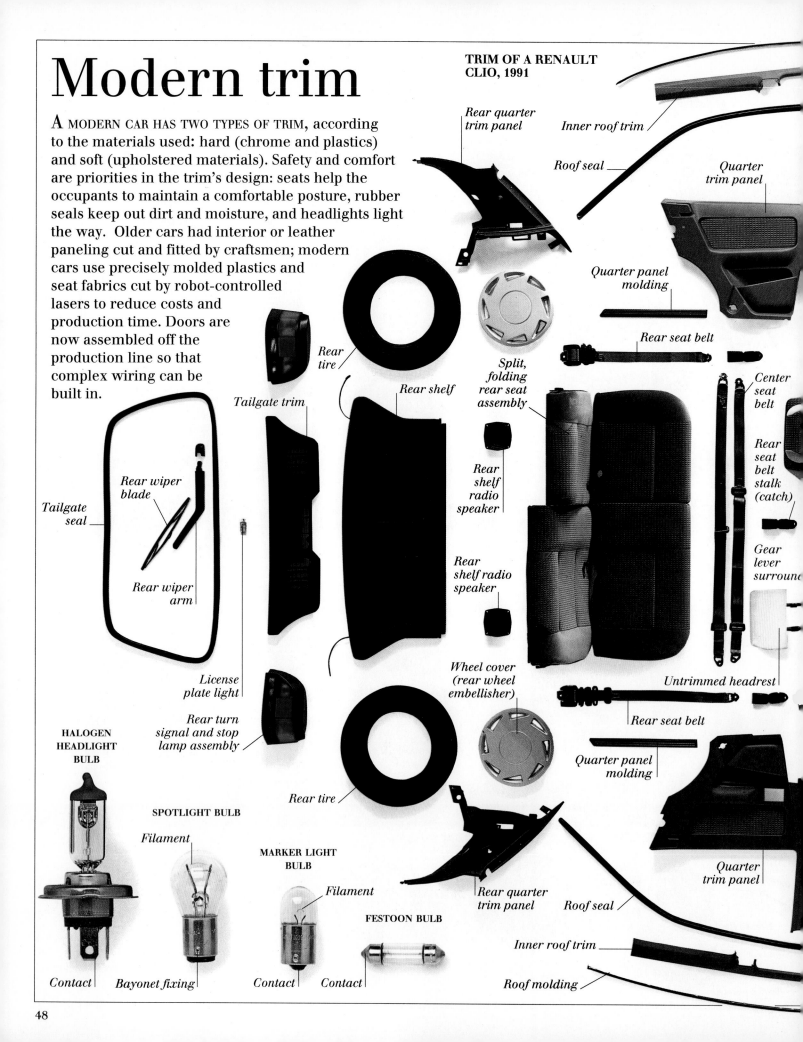

Rear quarter trim panel

Inner roof trim

Roof seal

Quarter trim panel

Quarter panel molding

Rear tire

Rear shelf

Split, folding rear seat assembly

Rear seat belt

Center seat belt

Tailgate trim

Rear shelf radio speaker

Rear seat belt stalk (catch)

Rear wiper blade

Gear lever surround

Tailgate seal

Rear shelf radio speaker

Rear wiper arm

License plate light

Wheel cover (rear wheel embellisher)

Untrimmed headrest

Rear turn signal and stop lamp assembly

Quarter panel molding

Rear seat belt

HALOGEN HEADLIGHT BULB

Rear tire

SPOTLIGHT BULB

Filament

Quarter trim panel

MARKER LIGHT BULB

Rear quarter trim panel

Roof seal

Filament

FESTOON BULB

Contact   *Bayonet fixing*   *Contact*   *Contact*

Inner roof trim

Roof molding

48

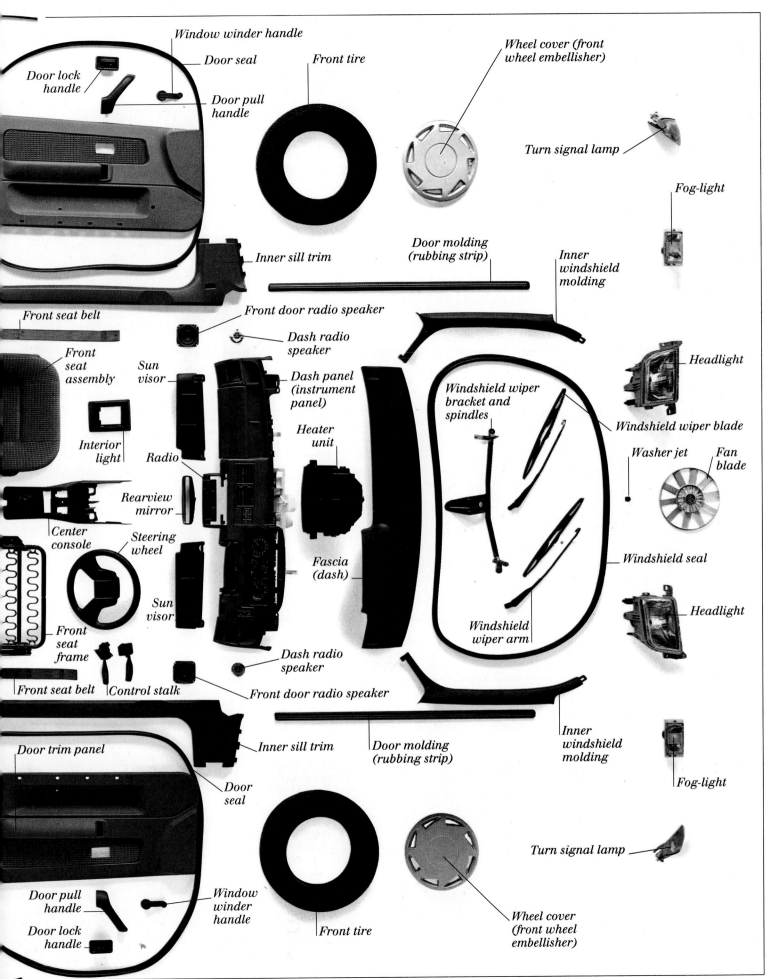

Door lock handle

Window winder handle

Door seal

Door pull handle

Front tire

Wheel cover (front wheel embellisher)

Turn signal lamp

Fog-light

Inner sill trim

Door molding (rubbing strip)

Inner windshield molding

Front seat belt

Front door radio speaker

Dash radio speaker

Headlight

Front seat assembly

Sun visor

Dash panel (instrument panel)

Windshield wiper bracket and spindles

Windshield wiper blade

Interior light

Radio

Heater unit

Washer jet

Fan blade

Rearview mirror

Center console

Steering wheel

Fascia (dash)

Windshield seal

Sun visor

Front seat frame

Dash radio speaker

Windshield wiper arm

Headlight

Front seat belt

Control stalk

Front door radio speaker

Inner sill trim

Door trim panel

Door seal

Door molding (rubbing strip)

Inner windshield molding

Fog-light

Door pull handle

Window winder handle

Door lock handle

Front tire

Wheel cover (front wheel embellisher)

Turn signal lamp

Coachbuilt cars

IN THE EARLY DAYS OF MOTORING, the purchasers of high-quality cars bought a chassis and then had a body built to their individual requirements by a master coachbuilder. Two examples are the Rolls-Royces on these pages. Early car bodies were built along principles similar to those used in horse-drawn carriage construction, although allowances had to be made for the extra stresses that made one year's use of a car equivalent to several of a horse-drawn carriage. For this reason, the wings, running boards, and wooden framework (which was covered by hand-formed wooden or metal paneling) were strengthened by iron stays made by blacksmiths. The bodywork was then finished with many coats of hand-applied paint and varnish.

ASH FRAME

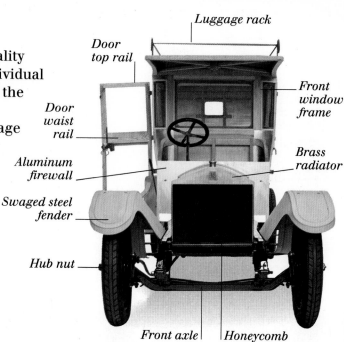

Luggage rack

Door top rail

Front window frame

Door waist rail

Brass radiator

Aluminum firewall

Swaged steel fender

Hub nut

Front axle

Honeycomb radiator core

1911 ROLLS-ROYCE SILVER GHOST "D" FRONT LIMOUSINE

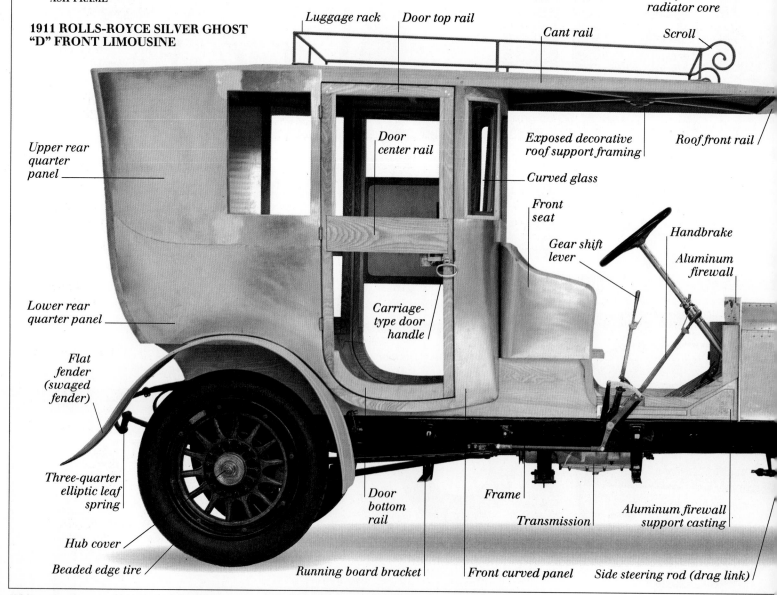

Luggage rack

Door top rail

Cant rail

Scroll

Upper rear quarter panel

Door center rail

Exposed decorative roof support framing

Roof front rail

Curved glass

Front seat

Handbrake

Lower rear quarter panel

Gear shift lever

Aluminum firewall

Carriage-type door handle

Flat fender (swaged fender)

Three-quarter elliptic leaf spring

Hub cover

Door bottom rail

Frame

Aluminum firewall support casting

Beaded edge tire

Running board bracket

Front curved panel

Transmission

Side steering rod (drag link)

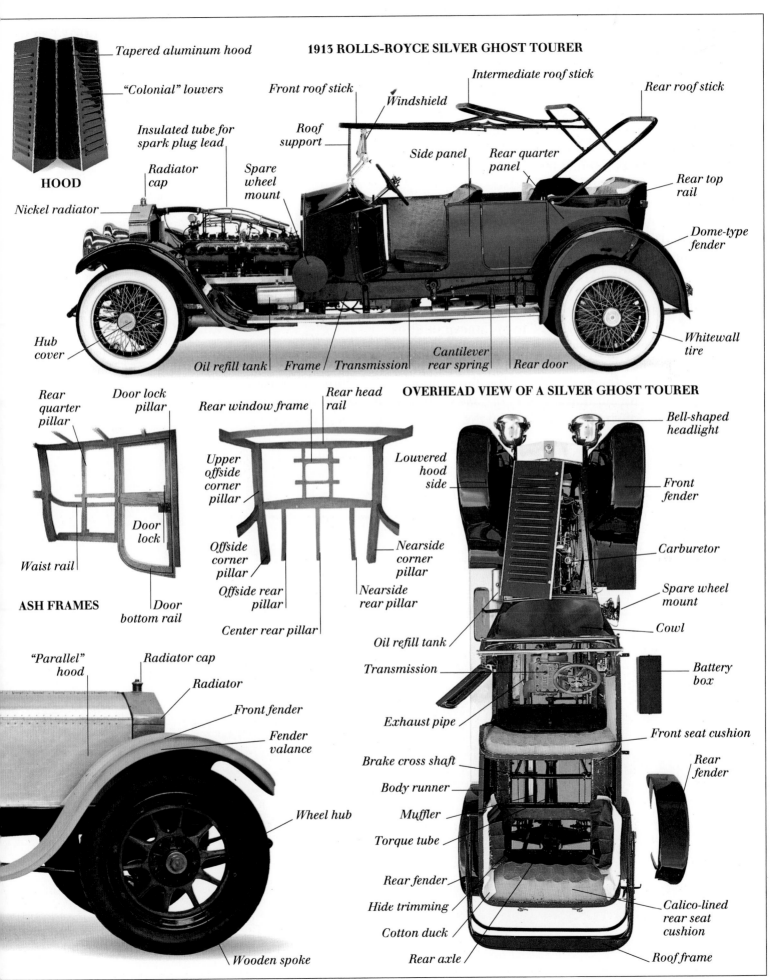

1913 ROLLS-ROYCE SILVER GHOST TOURER

Tapered aluminum hood

"Colonial" louvers

Front roof stick

Intermediate roof stick

Rear roof stick

Windshield

Insulated tube for spark plug lead

Roof support

Side panel

Rear quarter panel

Rear top rail

Radiator cap

Spare wheel mount

HOOD

Nickel radiator

Dome-type fender

Hub cover

Oil refill tank   Frame   Transmission

Cantilever rear spring

Rear door

Whitewall tire

Rear quarter pillar

Door lock pillar

Rear window frame

Rear head rail

OVERHEAD VIEW OF A SILVER GHOST TOURER

Upper offside corner pillar

Louvered hood side

Bell-shaped headlight

Front fender

Door lock

Carburetor

Waist rail

Offside corner pillar

Nearside corner pillar

Spare wheel mount

ASH FRAMES

Door bottom rail

Offside rear pillar

Nearside rear pillar

Cowl

Center rear pillar

Oil refill tank

Battery box

"Parallel" hood

Radiator cap

Radiator

Transmission

Exhaust pipe

Front seat cushion

Front fender

Brake cross shaft

Rear fender

Fender valance

Body runner

Muffler

Wheel hub

Torque tube

Rear fender

Hide trimming

Calico-lined rear seat cushion

Cotton duck

Rear axle

Roof frame

Wooden spoke

Cars assembled by hand

LATER COACHBUILT CARS, such as the 1932 Alvis shown here, combined traditional craftsmanship with elements of mass-production. Their bodies could be assembled by hand in large numbers by using standardized wooden components and mechanically pressed exterior metal panelwork. Where individually built bodies used timber cut to shape by craftsmen, other coachbuilt bodies were made using template-cut timber, which could be produced in greater quantities. Such developments enabled the costs of coachwork to be kept down. By the end of the 1930s, all-steel bodies had become virtually universal, and, by the end of the 1950s, the economic advantages of mass-production meant that the craft of coachbuilding became limited to the restoration of vintage vehicles and the production of exclusive cars.

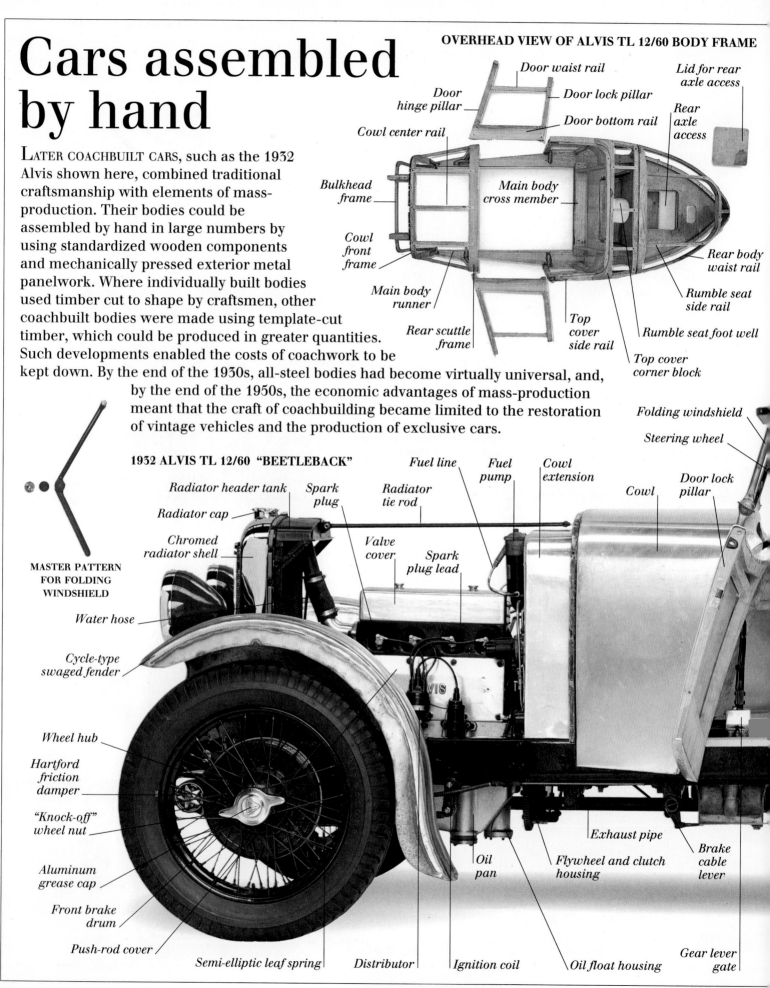

OVERHEAD VIEW OF ALVIS TL 12/60 BODY FRAME

Door waist rail
Lid for rear axle access
Door hinge pillar
Door lock pillar
Door bottom rail
Rear axle access
Cowl center rail
Bulkhead frame
Main body cross member
Cowl front frame
Rear body waist rail
Main body runner
Rumble seat side rail
Rear scuttle frame
Top cover side rail
Rumble seat foot well
Top cover corner block

Folding windshield
Steering wheel

MASTER PATTERN FOR FOLDING WINDSHIELD

1932 ALVIS TL 12/60 "BEETLEBACK"

Fuel line
Fuel pump
Cowl extension
Cowl
Door lock pillar
Radiator header tank
Spark plug
Radiator tie rod
Radiator cap
Chromed radiator shell
Valve cover
Spark plug lead
Water hose
Cycle-type swaged fender
Wheel hub
Hartford friction damper
"Knock-off" wheel nut
Aluminum grease cap
Exhaust pipe
Brake cable lever
Oil pan
Flywheel and clutch housing
Front brake drum
Push-rod cover
Semi-elliptic leaf spring
Distributor
Ignition coil
Oil float housing
Gear lever gate

52

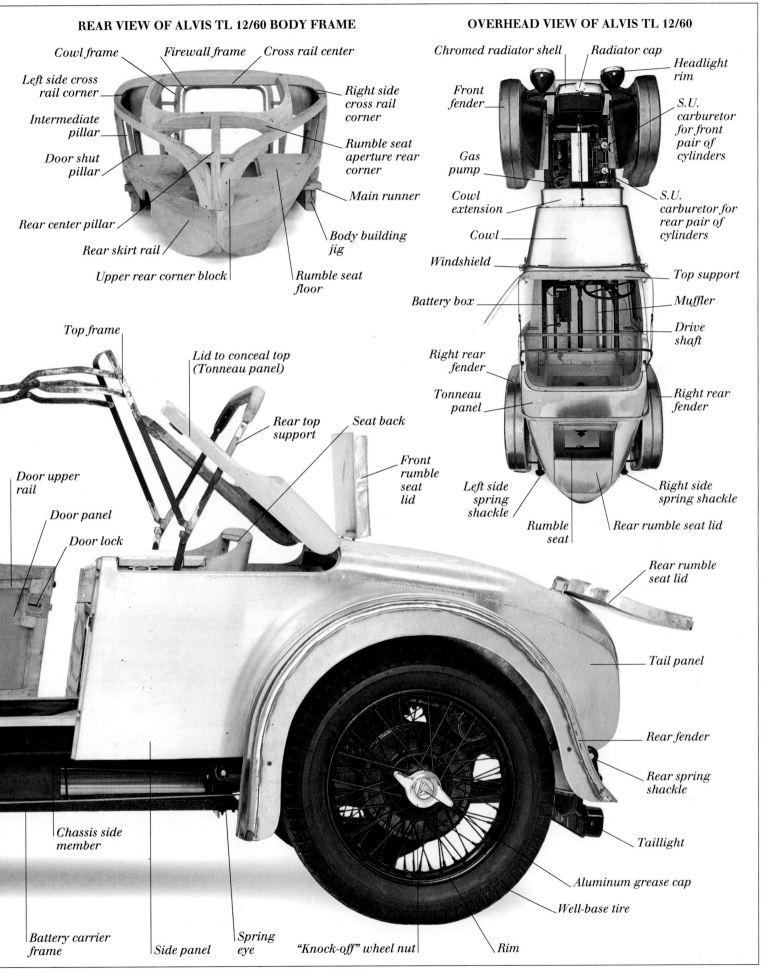

REAR VIEW OF ALVIS TL 12/60 BODY FRAME

Cowl frame

Firewall frame

Cross rail center

Left side cross rail corner

Right side cross rail corner

Intermediate pillar

Rumble seat aperture rear corner

Door shut pillar

Main runner

Rear center pillar

Body building jig

Rear skirt rail

Upper rear corner block

Rumble seat floor

OVERHEAD VIEW OF ALVIS TL 12/60

Chromed radiator shell

Radiator cap

Headlight rim

Front fender

S.U. carburetor for front pair of cylinders

Gas pump

Cowl extension

S.U. carburetor for rear pair of cylinders

Cowl

Windshield

Top support

Battery box

Muffler

Drive shaft

Right rear fender

Tonneau panel

Right rear fender

Left side spring shackle

Right side spring shackle

Rumble seat

Rear rumble seat lid

Top frame

Lid to conceal top (Tonneau panel)

Rear top support

Seat back

Front rumble seat lid

Door upper rail

Door panel

Door lock

Rear rumble seat lid

Tail panel

Chassis side member

Rear fender

Rear spring shackle

Taillight

Battery carrier frame

Aluminum grease cap

Side panel

Spring eye

"Knock-off" wheel nut

Well-base tire

Rim

53

Trim and upholstery

"TRIM" REFERS TO the embellishments of a car, such as the seats, windows, tires, and decoration. "Upholstery" refers to the soft materials used. Cars reached a peak of ostentation with the American models of the 1950s, like the Cadillac Eldorado. Such cars often had large amounts of chrome-plated metalwork and extravagantly upholstered interiors; some even had gold-plated "brightwork" (polished metalwork). Although seats originally used horsehair and individually pocketed springs, they are now usually made with foam filling, which can be molded to the required shape. Many luxury cars still use hand-stitched leather hides for their upholstery and matched wood veneers to trim their dashboards and door cappings.

FRONT VIEW OF CADILLAC ELDORADO, 1954

Radio antenna

Hood crest

Hood ornament

Rearview mirror

Windshield

Steering wheel

Spotlight and door mirror

Hood

Front fender

Headlight unit

Headlight surround

Chrome molding

Turn signal housing

Turn signal

Cross-ply whitewall tire

Overrider support

Grille upright

Bumper

Grille center bar

Overrider (Dagmar)

Vee motif

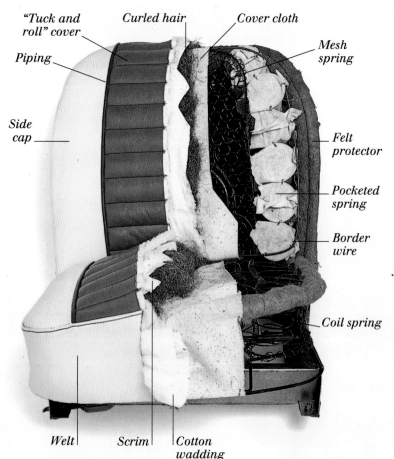

"Tuck and roll" cover

Curled hair

Cover cloth

Piping

Mesh spring

Side cap

Felt protector

Pocketed spring

Border wire

Coil spring

Welt

Scrim

Cotton wadding

SECTIONED TRADITIONAL SPRUNG SEAT

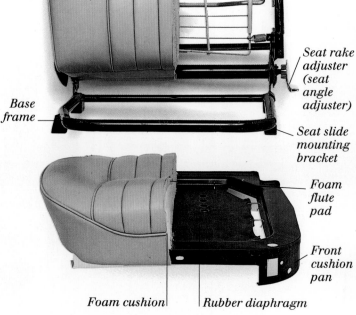

Headrest

Headrest insert panel

Back

Tubular frame

Wire framing

Support spring

Base frame

Seat rake adjuster (seat angle adjuster)

Seat slide mounting bracket

Foam flute pad

Front cushion pan

Foam cushion

Rubber diaphragm

SECTIONED MODERN SEAT

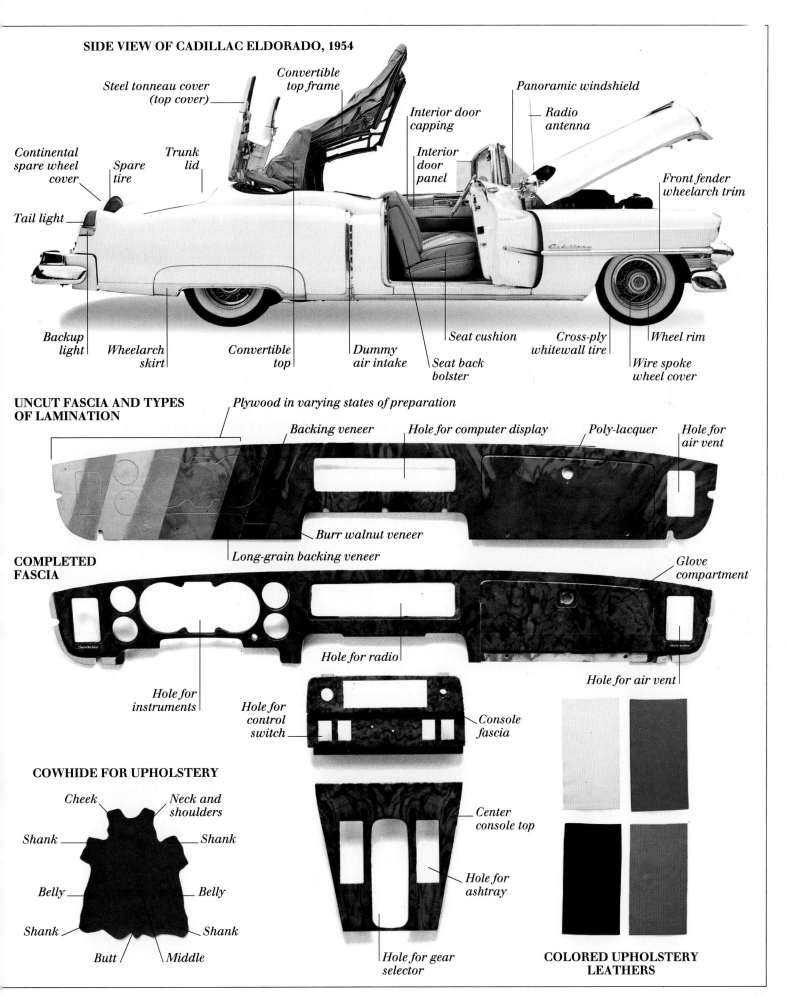

SIDE VIEW OF CADILLAC ELDORADO, 1954

Steel tonneau cover (top cover)

Convertible top frame

Interior door capping

Panoramic windshield

Radio antenna

Continental spare wheel cover

Spare tire

Trunk lid

Interior door panel

Front fender wheelarch trim

Tail light

Backup light

Wheelarch skirt

Convertible top

Dummy air intake

Seat back bolster

Seat cushion

Cross-ply whitewall tire

Wheel rim

Wire spoke wheel cover

UNCUT FASCIA AND TYPES OF LAMINATION

Plywood in varying states of preparation

Backing veneer

Hole for computer display

Poly-lacquer

Hole for air vent

Burr walnut veneer

Long-grain backing veneer

COMPLETED FASCIA

Glove compartment

Hole for instruments

Hole for radio

Hole for air vent

Hole for control switch

Console fascia

COWHIDE FOR UPHOLSTERY

Cheek

Neck and shoulders

Shank

Shank

Belly

Belly

Shank

Shank

Butt

Middle

Center console top

Hole for ashtray

Hole for gear selector

COLORED UPHOLSTERY LEATHERS

All-terrain vehicles

THE MODERN ALL-TERRAIN VEHICLE has its origins in the American military Jeep of the 1940s and the British Land Rover. Such vehicles have been used for a wide range of purposes, from safari travel to fire fighting. The principal special features of such cars—including four- or six-wheel drive, high ground clearance, and toughened braking, suspension, and transmission systems—are designed to enable driving under the most difficult off-road conditions. The vehicle shown here is equipped for safari travel and carries a comprehensive range of survival gear.

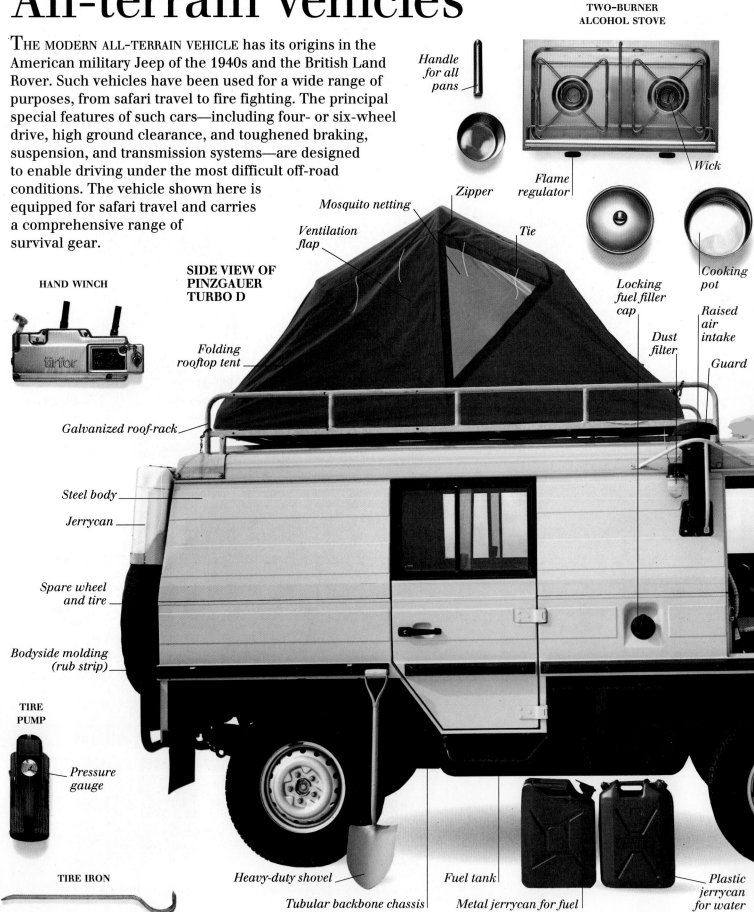

COOKING EQUIPMENT

TWO–BURNER ALCOHOL STOVE

Handle for all pans

Flame regulator

Wick

Cooking pot

HAND WINCH

Tirfor

Zipper

Mosquito netting

Ventilation flap

Tie

SIDE VIEW OF PINZGAUER TURBO D

Locking fuel filler cap

Dust filter

Raised air intake

Guard

Folding rooftop tent

Galvanized roof-rack

Steel body

Jerrycan

Spare wheel and tire

Bodyside molding (rub strip)

TIRE PUMP

Pressure gauge

TIRE IRON

Heavy-duty shovel

Tubular backbone chassis

Fuel tank

Metal jerrycan for fuel

Plastic jerrycan for water

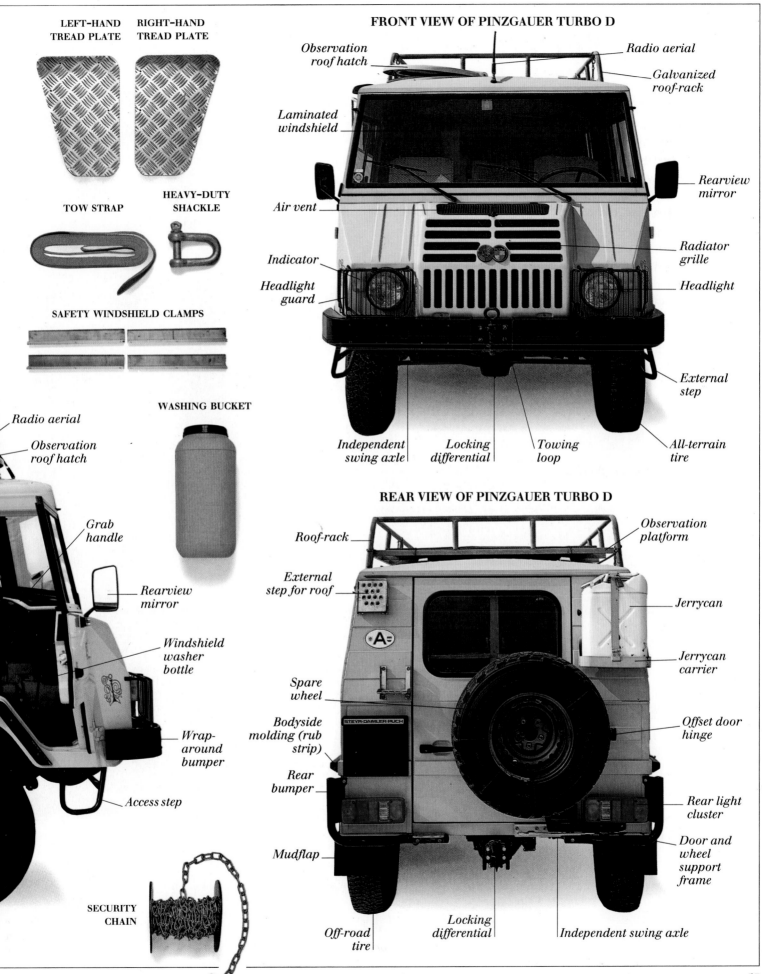

LEFT-HAND
TREAD PLATE

RIGHT-HAND
TREAD PLATE

TOW STRAP

HEAVY-DUTY
SHACKLE

SAFETY WINDSHIELD CLAMPS

WASHING BUCKET

Radio aerial

Observation
roof hatch

Grab
handle

Rearview
mirror

Windshield
washer
bottle

Wrap-
around
bumper

Access step

SECURITY
CHAIN

FRONT VIEW OF PINZGAUER TURBO D

Observation
roof hatch

Radio aerial

Galvanized
roof-rack

Laminated
windshield

Rearview
mirror

Air vent

Indicator

Radiator
grille

Headlight
guard

Headlight

External
step

Independent
swing axle

Locking
differential

Towing
loop

All-terrain
tire

REAR VIEW OF PINZGAUER TURBO D

Roof-rack

Observation
platform

External
step for roof

Jerrycan

Jerrycan
carrier

Spare
wheel

Offset door
hinge

Bodyside
molding (rub
strip)

Rear
bumper

Rear light
cluster

Mudflap

Door and
wheel
support
frame

Off-road
tire

Locking
differential

Independent swing axle

Racing cars

SINCE MOTORING BEGAN, racing cars have been a major focus of innovation in car design. Features that are now commonplace, such as disc brakes, turbochargers, and even safety belts, were used first on competition cars. Research into racing cars has contributed to a new understanding of engine performance, aerodynamics, and tire adhesion, and has led to the development of ultra-light materials such as carbon-fiber for car bodies. Like the 1937 Bugatti Type 57S below, today's Williams Formula One car has a low, streamlined body and an open cockpit. Unlike its forerunner, it also has a front wing that pushes the front wheels firmly on to the track, huge slick tires for extra grip, and electrical sensors that continually relay information to the pits about the car's performance.

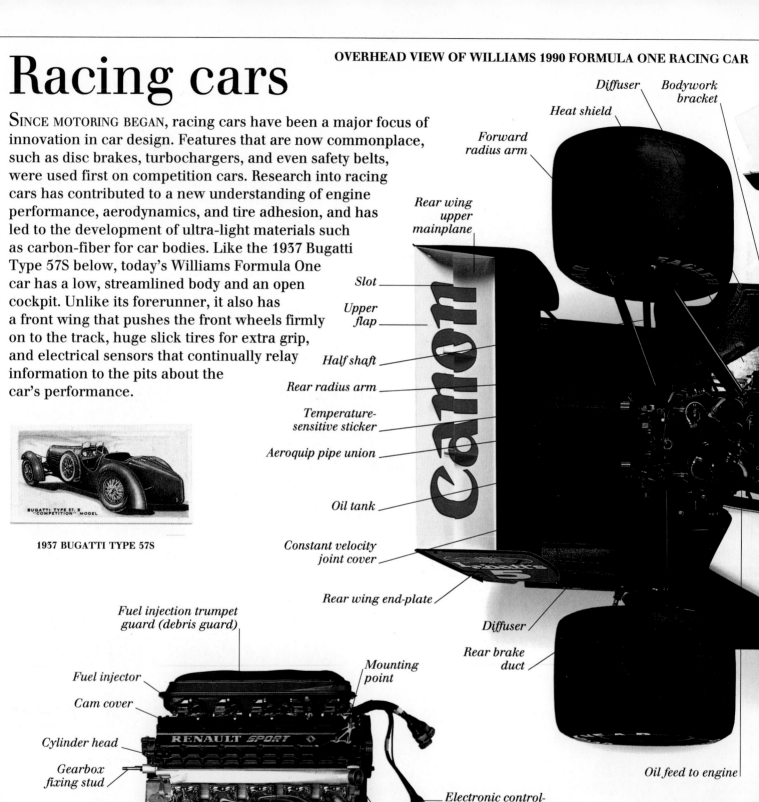

1937 BUGATTI TYPE 57S

Diffuser

Bodywork bracket

Heat shield

Forward radius arm

Rear wing upper mainplane

Slot

Upper flap

Half shaft

Rear radius arm

Temperature-sensitive sticker

Aeroquip pipe union

Oil tank

Constant velocity joint cover

Rear wing end-plate

Diffuser

Rear brake duct

Oil feed to engine

ENGINE COWLING

Dzus fastener

Fuel injection trumpet guard (debris guard)

Mounting point

Fuel injector

Cam cover

Cylinder head

Gearbox fixing stud

Electronic control-unit connector

Water outlet

Tail pipe

Stressed cylinder block

Harmonically-tuned exhaust pipe

RENAULT V10 RS1 ENGINE

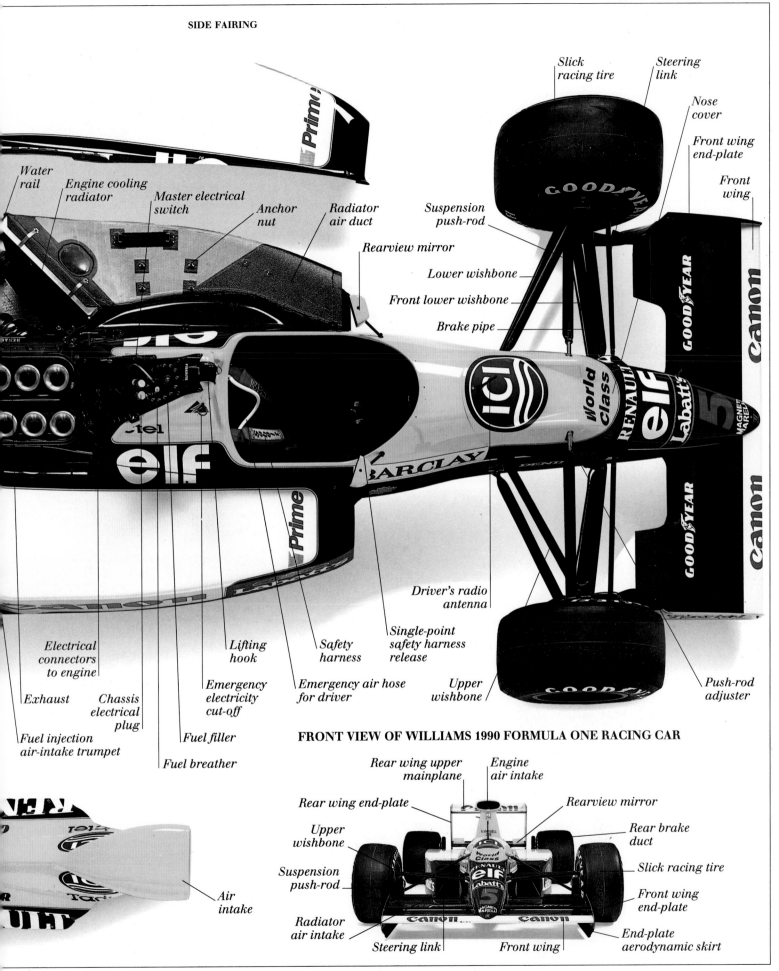

Slick racing tire

Steering link

Nose cover

Front wing end-plate

Front wing

Water rail

Engine cooling radiator

Master electrical switch

Anchor nut

Radiator air duct

Suspension push-rod

Rearview mirror

Lower wishbone

Front lower wishbone

Brake pipe

Driver's radio antenna

Single-point safety harness release

Upper wishbone

Push-rod adjuster

Electrical connectors to engine

Lifting hook

Safety harness

Emergency air hose for driver

Exhaust

Chassis electrical plug

Emergency electricity cut-off

Fuel filler

Fuel injection air-intake trumpet

Fuel breather

FRONT VIEW OF WILLIAMS 1990 FORMULA ONE RACING CAR

Rear wing upper mainplane

Engine air intake

Rear wing end-plate

Rearview mirror

Upper wishbone

Rear brake duct

Suspension push-rod

Slick racing tire

Radiator air intake

Front wing end-plate

Air intake

Steering link

Front wing

End-plate aerodynamic skirt

Index

A

Accelerator 21
Accelerator (throttle) pedal
Mercedes car 41
Oldsmobile trim 9
Renault Clio 46
Access panel 8
Access step 9
Acetylene generator 42
Acetylene headlight
Examples of 43
Mercedes car 31, 40
1906 Renault 8-9
Actuator rod 25
Adjustable carrier 21
Adjustable valve-seating 20
Adjuster bar 38
Adjuster bolt 38
Adjusting rod 38
A.E.I. (Automatic Electronic Ignition) unit 22
Aerodynamic windshield
Mazda RX-7 18
Renault Espace 32
Aeroquip pipe union 58
Air cleaner
Jaguar V12 engine 17
Renault Clio 46
Air compressor wheel 25
Air conditioning 26-27
Air conditioning compressor 16
Air conditioning compressor
Cooling and lubrication 27
Ford V6 24-valve engine 16
Air conditioning refrigerant pipe 16
Air filter
Air and gas flow in a turbocharger 24
Volkswagen Beetle 12
Airfoil-shaped metal strut 30
Air inlet
Jaguar V12 engine 17
Trier and Martin carburetor 21
Turbocharger 24-25
Air intake
Carburetors 20-21
Pinzgauer Turbo D 56
Williams Formula One car 59
Air intake vents 13
Air mixed with gasoline vapor 20
Air port 21
Air port chamber 20
Air scoop 12
Airscrew shield 30
Air tube 20
Air vent 57
Alloy wheel 46-47
All-terrain tire 57
All-terrain vehicles 56-57
Alternative engines 18-19
Alternator
Ford V6 12-valve engine 16
Jaguar V12 engine 17
Renault Clio 46
Wiring harness 43
Alternator belt 16
Alternator cooling fan 16
Alternator pulley 17
Aluminum alloy backing 18
Aluminum bulkhead 50
Aluminum bulkhead support casting 50
Aluminum firewall 50
Aluminum grease cap 52-53
Aluminum lid 22
Alvis body frame 52-53
Alvis TL 12/60 "Beetleback" 52-53
Anchor nut 59
Accessory drive belt 19
Ancillary drive pulley 17
Anti-dieseling valve 21
Antilock braking system 39
Anti-rattle pin 38
Anti-rattle spring 38
Anti-rattle washer 38
Anti-roll bar
Renault Clio 46-47
Volkswagen Beetle 12
Anti-surge baffle 16
Apex seal 19
Apex seal groove 19

Apex seal spring 19
Arm 13
Armature 22
Artillery wheel
Bordino Steam Carriage 6
Mercedes car 31
Panhard & Levassor 28
Wheels and tires 36
Ash frames 50-51
"A" spark gap 23
Aston Martin 26
Aston Martin dry sump 26-27
Aston Martin oil pump assembly 26
Atomizing air passage 21
Austin Healey grille 27
Autoclipse acetylene headlight 43
Automatic cylinder lubricator 14
Automatic transmission 30-31
Axle beam
Aston Martin dry sump 26-27
de Dion-Bouton 35
Axle torque cable 26
Axle tube 33

B

Back 54
Backing veneer 55
Back-lock motor 42
Back plate 38
Back release 42
Backrest release 42
Baffle 13
Baffle plate
Ford diesel engine 19
Surface carburetor 20
Bail handle
Headlights 43
Mercedes car 40
1906 Renault 8
Balance weight 17
Balancing drilling 19
Ball joint 32
Band brake
Brakes 38
de Dion-Bouton 35
Banjo bolt 25
Banjo fitting 25
Base coat color 44
Base frame 54
Base rubber 37
Base tank 27
Batteries 14
Battery 43
Battery box
Alvis TL 12/60 53
Rolls-Royce Tourer 51
Battery carrier 10
Battery carrier frame 53
Battery gauge 40
Battery strap 11
Bayonet fixing 48
Bead area 37
Bead core 37
Beaded edge tire
Leyat 30
Mercedes car 31
1906 Renault 8
Rolls-Royce Limousine 50
Bead heel 37
Bead protector ply 37
Bead sole 37
Bead toe 37
Bead wire 37
Bearing
Differential unit 32
Jaguar V12 engine 17
Macpherson strut 34
Power-assisted steering 33
Rack and pinion 33
Turbocharger 25
Bearing housing
Jaguar straight six engine 16
Parts of a supercharger 25
Bearing sleeve 10
Bedford cord upholstery 8
Bell crank 38
Bell housing 19
Bell-shaped headlight 51
Belly
Artillery wheel 36
Cowhide 55
Belt pulley 17
Belt shield 31

Belt tensioner 16
Benz, Karl 6
Benz Motorwagen 7
Benz plug 23
Bersey electric cab 14
Bevel gear
Benz Motorwagen 7
Crash gearbox 28
Four-wheel steering 33
Bevel gearing 40
Bevel pinion 10
"Bibendum" 36
Bi-block engine 9
Big end
Flat-four cylinder arrangement 12
Four-stroke cycle 15
Jaguar straight six engine 16
Trojan engine 14
Big-end bearing 7
Binding screw 23
Blade 13
Blanking plate 24
Bleriot acetylene headlight 43
Blind pull 8-9
Blinking screw 23
Body building jig 53
Body mount 10
Body runner 51-52
Body-side molding
Mazda RX-7 18
Pinzgauer Turbo D 56-57
Bodyshell
Renault Clio 44-45
Volkswagen Beetle 13
Bodywork 44-45
Cars assembled by hand 52
Coachbuilt cars 50
Racing cars 58
Volkswagen Beetle 13
Bodywork bracket 58
Bodywork of a Renault Clio 44-45
Bolt hole for hub 36
Bolt-on dumb iron 33
Bolt-on plate 36
Border wire 55
Bordino Steam Carriage 6-7
Bottom radiator hose 47
Bottom leaf 34
Bottom valve 34
Bowden speedometer 41
Boyce motometer 27
Bracing belt 37
Bracing cord 37
Brake adjuster-spring sleeve 26
Brake-and-gradient meter 40
Brake assembly 32
Brake back plate
Aston Martin dry sump 27
Renault Clio 46
Volkswagen Beetle 12
Brake band 38
Brake block 39
Brake cable 26
Brake cable lever 52
Brake calliper
Exploded disc brake 39
Modern disc brake 38
Renault Clio 47
Brake calliper fixing bolt 47
Brake calliper locking plate 47
Brake cross shaft
Panhard-system chassis 33
Rolls-Royce Tourer 51
Brake cylinder
Drum brake 38
Renault Clio 46-47
Brake disc
Exploded disc brake 39
Renault Clio 47
Brake drum
Alvis TL 12/60 52
Aston Martin dry sump 27
Band brake 38
Ford Model T 11-12
Leyat 30
Mercedes car 31
White Steam Car 14
Brake drum and hub 38
Brake duct 58-59
Brake hose 47
Brake lever
Benz Motorwagen 7
Daimler Maybach 31
Markus Motor Carriage 39
Rim brake 38
White Steam Car 14
Wraparound brake 38
Brake lining 38
Brake pad
Exploded disc brake 39
Modern disc brake 39
Renault Clio 47

Brake pedal
Mercedes car 31, 41
Oldsmobile bodywork 9
Renault Clio 46
Steam-powered Cugnot 6
Brake Perrot shaft 26
Brake pipe 59
Brake quadrant 7
Brake rod
Aston Martin dry sump 27
Band brake 38
Ford Model T 11
Oldsmobile chassis 9
Panhard-system chassis 33
Rim brake 38
Wraparound band brake 38
Brake rod adjuster 27
Brakes 38-39
Modern components 46
Brake power-assist servo 47
Brake shield 47
Brake shoe
Antilock braking system 39
Modern drum brake 38
Renault Clio 46
Brake shoe return-spring 38
Brass and vulcanite terminal 22
Brass bevel 8-9
Brass body 23
Brass cap 23
Brass casing 40
Brass housing for ignition cable 15
Brass mounting flange 41
Brass radiator 50
Brass rivet nut 23
Brass scrollwork 9
Brass strap 27
Brass terminal nut 23
Brass valve stem 37
British Automobile Association badge 8
British Royal Automobile Club badge 8
Broad lace trim 8-9
Broad, rough tire 6
Bronze driving gear 25
"B" spark terminal 23
Bucket seat 31
Bucket tappet 16
Bugatti Type 57S 58
Bulb horn
Ford Model T 10
Mercedes car 31
1906 Renault 9
Bulbs 48
Bumper
Cadillac Eldorado 54
Pinzgauer Turbo D 57
Renault Clio 44-45
Volkswagen Beetle 13
Bun lamp burner 11
Burr walnut veneer 55
Bush 29
Butt 55
Butterfly throttle spindle 20
Butterfly valve 21
Button-quilted upholstery 8
Butyl rubber 37
Bypass to pilot jet 20

C

Cable steel cord 37
Cable tire 36
Cadillac Eldorado 54-55
Calico-lined rear seat cushion 51
Cam 16
Cambered rear wheel 35
Cam cover
Jaguar straight six engine 16
Jaguar V12 engine 17
Renault VS10 RS1 engine 58
Cam follower
Ford diesel engine 19
Jaguar straight six engine 16
Jaguar V12 engine 17
Cam lobe 16
Camshaft
Humber engine 15
Jaguar straight six engine 16
Jaguar V12 engine 17
Camshaft chain 16
Camshaft sprocket 17
Camshaft timing gear 16
Candle lamp
Bordino Steam Carriage 7
Panhard & Levassor 28
Canopy 8-9

Cantilever rear spring 51
Cant rail 50
Carbide chamber 42
Carbon black 37
Carbon brush holder 22
Carburetors 20-21
Daimler engine 15
Ford Model T 11
Morgan Aero 35
Oldsmobile engine 8
Rolls-Royce Tourer 51
Drive shaft
Alvis TL 12/60 53
Panhard-system chassis 33
Carriage-type door handle 50
Carrier 39
Carrying fork 6
Cars assembled by hand 52-53
Casing for worm gearing 40
Cast alloy wheel 18
Cast aluminum wheel spider 8
Castle Three radiator 27
Catalytic converter
Modern engines 16
Renault Clio 46
Cataphoresic coating 44
Catch 43
Central carbon holder 22
Central electrode 23
Central shaft 29
Center console 49
Center console top 55
Center rear pillar 51
Center seat belt 48
Centring line 37
Chain sprocket
Aston Martin oil pump 26
Crash gearbox 28
Mercedes car 31
Champion priming plug 23
Channel steel chassis 31
Charge
Carburetors 20
Four-stroke cycle 15
Ignition systems 22
Modern engines 16
Power boosters 24
Chassis
Coachbuilt cars 50-51
First cars 6-7
Ford Model T 10
Mercedes car 31
Oldsmobile chassis 9
Panhard-system chassis 33
Pinzgauer Turbo D 56
Volkswagen Beetle 12
White Steam Car 14
Chassis attachment eye 34
Chassis electrical plug 59
Chassis frame 10
Chassis member 27
Chassis side member 53
Chassis tube and water tank 23
Chauffeur's seat 6
Cheek 55
Chevron-tread tire 8
Chimney 6
Chin spoiler 18
Choke adjusting screw 21
Choke butterfly plate 21
Choke tube 20-21
Chromed radiator shell 52-53
Chrome housing 43
Chrome molding 54
Chrome passivation 44
Chrome plating 19
Chrome trim strip 13
Circlip 32
Circumferential groove 37
Clear passage 37
Clevis 38
Clevis joint 21
Clincher wheel 11
Clip 33
Clock 40-41
Clutch 28-29
Markus Motor Carriage 39
Transmission systems 30
Clutch and flywheel 12
Clutch bell-housing 28
Clutch cable 46
Clutch center plate 47
Clutch housing 29
Clutch lever 39
Clutch pedal
Mercedes car 31, 41
Renault Clio 46
Clutch plate mounting hole 28
Clutch plates 30
Clutch pressure plate 47
Clutch throw-out bearing 47

Clutch release collar 29
Clutch release rod 28
Clutch slave cylinder 29
Clutch spring 29
Coachbuilt cars 50-51
Cogged drive belt 16
Coal hopper 6
Coil and wishbone suspension 34
Coil spring
Sprung seat 54
Suspension 34-35
"Colonial" louvers 51
Cowl
Alvis TL 12/60 52-53
Rolls-Royce Tourer 51
Cowl center rail 52
Cowl extension 52-53
Cowl frame 52-53
Cowl front frame 52
Combustion chamber 16
Compression ring
Ford diesel engine 19
Jaguar straight six engine 16
Compression stroke 15
Compressor housing 25
Compressor piston 16
Computer
Electrical systems 42-43
Modern bodywork 44
Computerized electric seat 42
Computerized ignition system 16
Computerized ignition coil 22
Computer wiring connection 25
Concave mirror 43
Condenser 14
Conducting bar 22
Confort Bibendum tire 36
Conical basin 20
Connecting pipe 20
Connecting rod
Bordino Steam Carriage 6
Flat-four cylinder arrangement 12
Four-stroke cycle 15
Jaguar straight six engine 16
Jaguar V12 engine 17
Markus Motor Carriage 39
Con-rod
Flat-four cylinder arrangement 12
Four-stroke cycle 15
Jaguar straight six engine 16
Jaguar V12 engine 17
Console fascia 55
Constant velocity joint cover 58
Contact 48
Contact-breaker cover 22
Contact-breaker spring 22
Continental spare wheel cover 55
Continuously variable transmission 30
Control lever for butterfly valve 20
Control harness 42
Control rod 33
Control stalk 49
Control valve 34
Control valve wiring harness 33
Cooking equipment 56
Coolant passage 18
Coolant rail 17
Cooling 26-27
Cooling fan 17
Cooling fin 24
Cooling tank 7
Cooling water jacket 25
Cooling water tank 7
Copper band 23
Copper cooling fin 23
Copper tube radiator 27
Copper washer 23
Copper wire 23
Cord 38
Cork float
Magnetic fuel gauge 41
Surface carburetor 20
Corner block 53
Corner brace 53
Corner pillar 51
Corner seal 19
Corner seal insert 19
Corner seal spring 19
Cotton duck 51
Cotton wadding 54
Countershaft 26
Countershaft band brake 28
Countershaft gear 26

- Counterweight
  - Cox Atmos carburetor 21
  - Flat-four cylinder arrangement 12
  - Four-stroke cycle 15
  - Jaguar V12 engine 17
  - Output shaft 19
  - Trojan engine 14
  - V12 cylinder arrangement 17
- Coupling 25
- Cover cloth 54
- Cover for distributor 22
- Cover locating spring 22
- Cover plate 29
- Cowey recording speed indicator 40
- Cowhide 55
- Cox Atmos carburetor 21
- Crank 25
- Crankcase
  - Daimler Maybach 31
  - Humber engine 15
  - Jaguar straight six engine 16
  - Jaguar V12 engine 17
  - Morgan Aero 35
  - Oldsmobile engine 8
  - Trojan engine 14
- Crankcase breather 26
- Cranked lever 31
- Crank handle 11
- Crankpin 15
- Crankshaft
  - Benz Motorwagen 7
  - Flat-four cylinder arrangement 12
  - Four-stroke cycle 15
  - Oldsmobile engine 8
  - Straight four cylinder arrangement 17
- Crankshaft bolt hole 28
- Crankshaft counterweight 16
- Crankshaft pulley 16
- Crash gearbox 28
- Cross-member
  - Alvis body frame 52
  - Ford Model T 10-11
- Cross-ply casing 36
- Cross-ply tire 36
- Cross-ply whitewall tire 54-55
- Cross rail center 53
- Cross rail corner 53
- Cross shaft 28
- Cross tube 26
- Crown 37
- Crown ply 37
- Crown wheel
  - Benz Motorwagen 7
  - Differential unit 32
  - Ford Model T 10
  - Panhard-system chassis 33
- Curled hair 54
- Curved glass 50
- Curved panel 50
- Cushion pan 54
- Cycle-type swaged fender 52
- Cycle fender 26
- Cyclometer 40-41
- Cylinder
  - Early engines 14-15
  - Morgan Aero 35
  - Oldsmobile engine 8
- Cylinder block 11
- Cylinder head
  - Daimler engine 15
  - Jaguar straight six engine 16
  - Jaguar V12 engine 17
  - Oldsmobile engine 8
  - Renault V10 RS1 engine 58
- Cylinder liner 16
- Cylinder wall 15

D

- Dagmar 54
- Daimler double-sleeve valve engine 15
- Daimler, Gottlieb 6
- Daimler Maybach 31
- Damper 20
- Damper body 35
- Damper spring 34
- Dash 49
- Dashboard
  - Bordino Steam Carriage 7
  - Ford Model T 10
  - Markus Motor Carriage 39
  - 1906 Renault 9
- Dashboard gauge 40
- Dashboard radiator 8-9
- Dash harness 42
- Dashboard
  - Renault Clio 49
  - Wiring harness 43
- Dash pot 21
- Dash radio speaker 49
- Dash speaker 43
- Debris guard 58
- de Dietrich radiator 27
- de Dion, Albert 6
- de Dion-Bouton 35
- de Dion suspension 34
- Degreased bare metal 44
- Delahaye plug 23
- Detachable rim 11
- Diaphragm
  - Modern seat 54
  - Weber carburetor 21
- Diesel fuel injection system 24
- Differential 33
- Differential gear 28
- Differential gear unit 32
- Differential housing 10
- Differential unit 32
- Diffuser 58
- Digital instrument panel 40
- Dimple 37
- Dipstick and oil-filler tube 31
- Dipstick tube 18
- Disc 38
- Disc brake 38-39
  - Racing cars 58
- Distributor
  - Alvis TL 12/60 52
  - Jaguar straight six engine 16
  - Jaguar V12 engine 17
  - Renault Clio 47
- Distributor body 22
- Distributor cap 22
- Distributor contact 22
- Distributor drive shaft 17
- Distributor dust cover 22
- Distributor fixing point 18
- Distributor rotor arm 22
- Division 9
- Dome-type fender 51
- Door 45
- Door and wheel support frame 57
- Door bottom rail
  - Alvis bodyframe 52
  - Ash frames 51
  - Rolls-Royce Limousine 50
- Door capping 55
- Door catch 13
- Door center rail 50
- Door glass 44
- Door handle
  - Renault Clio 44
  - Volkswagen Beetle 13
- Door hinge 45
- Door hinge pillar 52
- Door key and lock 44
- Door lock
  - Alvis TL 12/60 53
  - Ash frames 51
  - Renault Clio 44
- Door lock handle 49
- Door lock pillar
  - Alvis TL 12/60 52
  - Ash frames 51
- Door mirror 54
- Door molding 49
- Door panel
  - Alvis TL 12/60 53
  - Cadillac Eldorado 55
- Door pull handle 49
- Door radio speaker 42
- Door seal 49
- Door shut pillar 53
- Door top rail 50
- Door trim panel 49
- Door upper rail 53
- Door waist rail
  - Alvis bodyframe 52
  - Rolls-Royce Limousine 50
- Dowel 36
- Drag link
  - Ford Model T 11
  - Panhard-system chassis 33
  - Rolls-Royce Limousine 50
  - White Steam Car 14
- Drain 20
- Drain plug
  - de Dion-Bouton 35
  - Ford Model T 11
  - Multi-plate clutch 29
  - Parts of a supercharger 25
  - Radiators 27
  - Solex Carburetor 20
- Drain tap
  - Peugeot (1896) 23
  - Radiators 27
  - Surface carburetor 20
- Drip-feed acetylene generator 42
- Drip-feed oiler 41
- Drive belt
  - Benz Motorwagen 7
  - Continuously variable transmission 30
  - Electric seat 42
  - Ford V6 24-valve engine 16
- Drive cable
  - Bowden speedometer 41
  - Electric fuel gauge 40
  - Electric seat 42
- Drive flange 27
- Drive gears 25
- Driven member 29
- Driven plates 28-29
- Driven pulley 7
- Drive plate 17
- Drive point 18
- Drive pulley 39
- Driver's radio aerial 59
- Driver's seat
  - Bordino Steam Carriage 7
  - Markus Motor Carriage 39
- Drive shaft
  - Crash gearbox 28
  - Four-wheel-drive running gear 32
  - Renault Clio 47
  - Volkswagen Beetle 12
- Drive shaft trunnion 32
- Drive wheel 39
- Driving belt 31
- Drive chain
  - Benz Motorwagen 7
  - Mercedes car 31
  - Peugeot (1896) 23
- Driving dog 29
- Driving plate 28
- Driving plates 29
- Driving pulley 7
- Driving seat 31
- Driving sprocket 7
- Driving stud 25
- Drop arm
  - Ford Model T 11
  - White Steam Car 14
- Drop-down window 6
- Drop glass 13
- Dropped rear axle 31
- Drum brakes 38
- Dumb iron
  - Mercedes car 31
  - Panhard & Levassor 28
  - 1906 Renault 8
  - White Steam Car 14
- Dummy air intake 55
- Dummy front door 11
- Dust cover 32-33, 34
- Dust shroud 12
- Dust filter 56
- Dzus fastener 58

E

- Early engines **14-15**
- Earthed electrode 23
- Eccentric rotor journal 19
- Eccentric shaft 19
- Elapsed speed and distance indicator 40
- Electrical systems **42-43**
- Electric cars 14
- Electric choke 21
- Electric choke assembly 21
- Electric fuel gauge 40
- Electric fuel pump 6
- Electric horn
  - Aston Martin 26
  - Morgan Aero 35
- Electric seat 42
- Electric window motor 45
- Electromagnetic drive-pulley 27
- Electronic control-unit connector 58
- Electronic ignition system 22
- Electronic ignition unit 47
- Elegance and utility **8-9**
- Elliott steering knuckle 8
- Embellisher 49
- Emblem 27
- Emergency air hose for driver 59
- Emergency electricity cut-off 59
- End casing 24-25
- End-plate 58-59
- End-plate aerodynamic skirt 59
- Engine air intake 59
- Engine bearer 15
- Engine block 19
- Engine cooling radiator 59
- Engine cover
  - Oldsmobile bodywork 9
  - Volkswagen Beetle 13
- Engine cover handle 9
- Engine cowling 58
- Engine lid 13
- Engine lifting bracket 19
- Engine management computer 43
- Engine mount 26
- Engine oil tank 40
- Engine plate 35
- Engines **14-19**
  - Bordino Steam Carriage 6
  - Daimler Maybach 31
  - Leyat 30
  - Markus Motor Carriage 39
  - Oldsmobile engine 8
  - Panhard-system chassis 33
  - Peugeot (1896) 23
  - 1906 Renault 9
  - Renault Clio 46-47
  - Renault V10 RS1 58
  - Volkswagen Beetle 12
- Engine timing gear 8
- Excess fuel return 21
- Excess fuel return pipe 24-25
- Exhaust
  - Ford diesel engine 19
  - Modern components 46-47
  - Williams Formula One racing car 59
- Exhaust downpipe
  - Aston Martin 26
  - Renault Clio 46
- Exhaust gas recirculation valve 16
- Exhaust heat shield 17
- Exhaust manifold
  - Jaguar V12 engine 17
  - 1906 Renault 9
  - Renault Clio 47
- Exhaust pipe
  - Alvis TL 12/60 52
  - Morgan Aero 35
  - Oldsmobile engine 8
  - Panhard & Levassor 28
  - Panhard-system chassis 33
  - Rolls-Royce Tourer 51
  - White Steam Car 14
- Exhaust port
  - Four-stroke cycle 15
  - Wankel engine 19
  - Wankel rotary cycle 18
- Exhaust muffler box 26
- Exhaust stroke 15
- Exhaust valve
  - Four-stroke cycle 15
  - Jaguar straight six engine 16
  - Jaguar V12 engine 17
- Extension housing 30
- External step 57
- Extra-fort tire 36

F

- Fan
  - Jaguar straight six engine 16
  - Leyat 30
- Fan blade 49
- Fan bracket 15
- Fan control dial 40
- Fan drive shaft 17
- Fan motor
  - Renault Clio 47
  - Wiring harness 43
- Fan motor support bracket 47
- Fascia
  - Renault Clio 49
  - Trim and upholstery 55
- Fascia air vent 40
- Fastening to frame 38
- Fast/idle adjusting screw 21
- Feed for ignition burners 28
- Felloe 36
- Felt protector 54
- Fender
  - Alvis TL 12/60 52-53
  - Cadillac Eldorado 54
  - Coachbuilt cars 50-51
  - Daimler Maybach 31
  - Elegance and utility 8-9
  - Ford Model T 10-11
  - Leyat 30
  - Morgan Aero 35
  - 1906 Renault 8
  - Peugeot (1896) 23
  - Rolls-Royce Tourer 51
  - Volkswagen Beetle 13
  - Williams Formula One racing car 59
- Fender eye bolt 11
- Fender piping 13
- Fender stay 9
- Fender valance
  - Alvis TL 12/60 53
  - Rolls-Royce Limousine 51
- Field coil 25
- Filament 48
- Filler neck 35
- Filter cap 31
- Fin 27
- Final drive **32-33**
- Final drive and gearbox 12
- Final-drive housing 33
- Final-drive sprocket 7
- Firewall frame 52-53
- Fire extinguisher mounting bracket 42
- Fire-tube boiler 6
- First cars **6-7**
- Fitting line 37
- Fixed gear 18-19
- Fixing bracket 20
- Fixing screw 43
- Fixing stud 24
- Flame regulator 56
- Flange
  - Electric fuel gauge 40
  - Spark plugs 23
  - Surface carburetor 20
- Flared fender 35
- Flash steam generator 14
- Flat-four cylinder arrangement 12
- Flat-four engine 12
- Flat fender 50
- Flat twin engine 30
- Flexible brass conduit 41
- Flexible bush 35
- Flitch (reinforcing plate) 33
- Flitch-plated wooden chassis 14
- Float
  - Carburetors 20-21
  - Electric fuel gauge 40
- Float arm 40
- Float chamber
  - Carburetors 20-21
  - Daimler Maybach 31
- Float-chamber lid 20
- Float feed chamber 20
- Float needle 20
- Float-needle valve 20
- Floor catch 41
- Floor pan 12
- Fluid filling cap 27
- Fluid reservoir 34
- Flywheel
  - Benz Motorwagen 7
  - Early engines 14-15
  - Friction clutch 28
  - Markus Motor Carriage 39
  - Oldsmobile engine 8
  - Panhard-system chassis 33
  - Renault Clio 47
- Flywheel and clutch housing 52
- Flywheel cover 39
- Flywheel housing 39
- Flywheel with balance weight 19
- Foam cushion 54
- Foam flute pad 54
- Fog-light
  - Renault Clio 45, 49
  - Wiring harness 43
- Fog-light wiring harness 43
- Footboard 7
- Ford Cosworth V6 12-valve engine 16
- Ford Cosworth V6 24-valve engine 16
- Ford, Henry 10
- Ford Model T 10-11
- Ford turbocharged diesel engine 19
- Forecarriage
  - Bordino Steam Carriage 7
  - Markus Motor Carriage 39
- Forked connecting-rod 14
- Fork mounting 43
- Four-stroke cycle 15
- Four-wheel-drive
  - All-terrain vehicles 56
  - Final drive and steering 32
- Four-wheel-drive running gear 32
- Four-wheel-steering rack 32-33
- Frame
  - Markus Motor Carriage 39
  - Steam-powered Cugnot 7
- Frame head 12
- Friction band 38
- Friction clutch 28
- Front axle
  - Ford Model T 10
  - Leyat 30
  - Mercedes car 40
  - Panhard-system chassis 33
  - 1906 Renault 8-9
  - Rolls-Royce Limousine 50
- Front axle beam 26
- Front harness 43
- Front spring
  - Aston Martin dry sump 27
  - Oldsmobile chassis 9
- Front-wheel drive 32
- Fuel/air intake pipe 9
- Fuel breather 59
- Fuel cap 44
- Fuel feed
  - Carburetors 20-21
  - Diesel fuel injection 24
  - Gasoline fuel injection 25
- Fuel filler 59
- Fuel filler cap 12
- Fuel filler neck 12
- Fuel gauge 41
- Fuel injection
  - Carburetors 20
  - Modern engines 16
  - Power boosters 24-25
  - Renault V10 RS1 engine 58
- Fuel injection air-intake trumpet 59
- Fuel injection management harness 43
- Fuel injection trumpet guard 58
- Fuel injector nozzle 17
- Fuel inlet 20, 21
- Fuel inlet pipe 20
- Fuel jet 21
- Fuel-level gauge 40
- Fuel line 52
- Fuel pipe 17
- Fuel pressure regulator 25
- fuel pump 52-53
- Fuel rail 25
- Fuel sediment bowl 11
- Fuel supply to burners 23
- Fuel tank
  - Benz Motorwagen 7
  - Panhard & Levassor 28
  - Panhard-system chassis 33
  - Pinzgauer Turbo D 56
  - Renault Clio 46
  - Volkswagen Beetle 12
  - White Steam Car 14
- Fuel tank filler neck 46
- Fuel tank sender unit 12
- Full-elliptic leaf spring 6-7
- Full-elliptic steering spring 9
- Full-speed steel pinion 22
- Fuse board assembly 42
- Fuse box 42
- Fuselage 30

G

- Gasket 21
- Gas chamber 20-21
- Gasoline fuel injection system 25
- Gauze 21
- Gear band 8
- Gearbox **28-29**
  - Coachbuilt cars 50-51
  - Electric seat 42
  - Ford Model T 11
  - Four-wheel-drive running gear 32
  - Panhard-system chassis 33
  - Renault Clio 47
  - Transmission systems 30
  - Volkswagen Beetle 12
- Gearbox and backrest adjustment motor 42
- Gearbox and final drive 12
- Gearbox casing
  - Manual gearbox 29
  - Continuously variable transmission 30
- Gearbox fixing stud 58
- Gearbox spline 28
- Gearbox tailpiece 29
- Gear-change rod 47
- Gear housing 30
- Gear knob 29
- Gearshift lever
  - Crash gearbox 28
  - Manual gearbox 29
  - Mercedes car 31
  - 1906 Renault 9
  - Renault Clio 46
  - Rolls-Royce Limousine 50
- Gear lever gate 52
- Gear lever knob 12
- Gear lever surround 48
- Gears
  - Clutch and gearbox 28-29
  - Transmission systems 30
- Gear selector fork 29
- Gear selector linkage 28
- Generator mounting opening 26
- Gilled tube element 27
- Gilled tube radiator 33
- Gland nut 23
- Glass-insulated plug 23
- Glass insulator 23
- Glove compartment 55

Grab handle
  Mercedes car 40
  Pinzgauer Turbo D 57
Grease nipple 27
Greaser 11
Grille center bar 54
Grilles 27
Grille upright 54
Groove for rope starter 7
Guard 56
Guide 21

H

Half-shaft
  Ford Model T 10
  Williams Formula One
    car 58
Half-speed gunmetal
  pinion 22
Halogen headlight bulb 48
Hand-assembled cars 52-53
Handbrake
  Ford Model T 11
  Mercedes car 31
  1906 Renault 9
  Renault Clio 46
  Rolls-Royce Limousine 50
  Volkswagen 13
Handbrake control shaft 10
Handbrake quadrant 11
Handbrake warning light 41
Hand-operated control for
  mixing valve 20
Hand throttle 41
Hand winch 56
Hard trim 48
Harmonically-tuned exhaust
  pipe 58
Hartford friction damper 52
Hartford shock absorber 26
Haystack boiler 6
Head containing magnet 41
Headlight
  Bordino Steam Carriage 7
  Bulbs 48
  Electrical systems 42-43
  Ford Model T 10-11
  Morgan Aero 35
  Pinzgauer Turbo D 57
  Renault Clio 45, 49
Headlight rim
  Alvis TL 12/60 53
  Ford Model T 11
Headlight shell 11
Headlight surround 54
Headlight unit
  Cadillac Eldorado 54
  Volkswagen Beetle 13
Head rail 51
Headrest
  Mazda RX-7 18
  Modern seat 54
  Renault Clio 45, 48
Headrest insert panel 54
Head restraint motor 42
Heater 41
Heater control 40
Heater unit 49
Heat exchanger 12
Heating element contacts 44
Heat-resistant lining 28
Heat shield 58
Helical port 24
Helical suspension spring 31
Hide trimming 51
High-pressure cylinder 14
High-tension ignition
  lead 11
High-tension lead 22
High-tension lead
  connection 22
Hinge 43
Hinged lid 9
Hollow regulating float 21
Honeycomb radiator 26-27
Honeycomb radiator core 50
Hood
  Cadillac Eldorado 54
  Coachbuilt cars 51
  Ford Model T 11
  1906 Renault 9
  Renault Clio 45
  Volkswagen Beetle 12-13
Hood bag 18
Hood catch
  1906 Renault 8
  Renault Clio 45
Hood clip 11
Hood cover 55
Hood cover side rail 52
Hood crest 54
Hood hinge
  Renault Clio 45
  Volkswagen Beetle 13
Hood lid 53
Hood ornament 54
Hood-release cable 45
Hood-release handle 13
Hood rest 40

Hood strap 26
Hood support 9
Horizontal engine 39
Horn
  Ford Model T 11
  Wiring harness 43
Horn bulb 11
Horse-drawn carriage
  Coachbuilt cars 50
  Wheels and tires 36
Hot-water inlet 21
Hot-water jacket 21
Hot-water outlet 21
Housing 33
Housing for electric
  motors 14
Hub
  Alvis TL 12/60 52
  Aston Martin dry sump 27
  Benz Motorwagen 7
  Bordino Steam Carriage 6
  1906 Renault 8
  Renault Clio 47
  Rolls-Royce Limousine 51
  Wheels and tires 36
Hub and brake drum 46
Hub bearing 47
Hub bolt 10
Hub brake shoe 10
Hubcap
  Cadillac Eldorado 55
  Daimler Maybach 31
  de Dion-Bouton 35
  Ford Model T 11
  Mercedes car 31
  1906 Renault 8
  Renault Clio 46
Hub carrier 47
Hub center 37
Hub cover 50-51
Hub nut
  Renault Clio 46
  Rolls-Royce Limousine 50
Hub seal 46
Humber engine 15
Hydraulic cylinder 34
Hydraulic shock absorber 34

I

Idle control valve 16
Ignition advance and
  retard 41
Ignition amplifier 17
Ignition burner 23
Ignition burner base 31
Ignition burner casing 31
Ignition coil 52
Ignition wire 30
Ignition lever 10
Ignition switch
  Electronic ignition 22
  Mercedes car 41
  Oldsmobile bodywork 9
Ignition systems 22-23
Ignition tube 23
Impeller
  Ford diesel engine 19
  Turbocharger 24-25
  Water pump 19
Independent portal swing
  axle 57
Independent sliding-pillar
  suspension 35
Indicator assembly 48
Indicator housing 54
Indicator lamp
  Renault Clio 49
  Wiring harness 43
Indicator lamp harness 43
Indicator lens 13
Indicator needle 40-41
Indicator warning light 41
Induction stroke 15
Injector nozzle 24-25
Intake manifold
  Daimler engine 15
  Jaguar V12 engine 17
  Morgan Aero 35
Intake manifold tract 17
Inlet passage 24
Intake port
  Daimler engine 15
  Humber engine 15
  Parts of a supercharger 24
Inlet rotor
  Ford diesel engine 19
  Turbocharger 25
Intake track 19
Inlet turbine 25
Intake valve
  Four-stroke cycle 15
  Humber engine 15
  Jaguar V12 engine 17
Inner lining 34
Inner sun wheel 32
Inner tube 34
Input shaft
  Automatic transmission 31
  Friction clutch 28

Inspection window 23
Instrument panel 49
Instrument panel
  assembly 42
Instruments 40-41
Insulated tube for plug
  lead 51
Insulator 23
Intake manifold 47
Intake pipe 7
Intake port 18
Interior light 49
Intermediate housing 18
Internal combustion engine
  First cars 6
Iron tire 6

J

Jaguar straight six engine 16
Jaguar V12 engine 17
Jeep 56
Jerrycan 56-57
Jerrycan carrier 57
Jet 20-21
Jet carrier 20
Jet carrier cover 21
Jet lever 20
Jockey pulley 31
Journal 19
Hose clamp 27
Jump seat 9
Junk ring 15

K

Key 22
King pin
  Ford Model T 10
  Macpherson strut 34
King pin greaser 40
KLG spark plug 23
Knock 36
"Knock-off" nut 36
"Knock-off" wheel nut
  Alvis TL 12/60 52-53
  Aston Martin dry sump 27
Knurled collar 40-41
Knurled outer body 23

L

Laminated propeller 30
Laminated windshield 57
Lamp bracket
  1906 Renault 8
  White Steam Car 14
Lamp cluster 13
Landau body 6
Landau iron 6
Land Rover 56
Large chamber 34
Lateral groove 37
Layshaft gear 29
Leaf 34
Leaf spring
  Ford Model T 10
  Friction clutch 28
  Markus Motor Carriage 39
  Suspension 34
Leather gaiter 35
Leather hood 6
Leather upholstery 9
Leather valance 9
Lenoir, Etienne
  Early engines 14
  First cars 6
Level gauge 21
Leyat 9
Leyden jar terminal 23
License plate
  Ford Model T 10
  Volkswagen Beetle 13
License plate lamp
  Renault Clio 48
  Volkswagen Beetle 13
  Wiring harness 42
Lid for carbide chamber 42
Lid for rear axle access 52
Lid to conceal hood 53
Lifting handle 8
Lifting hook 9
Light-diffusing glass 43
Light switch 11
Lighting switch 42
Link 38
Lip 37
Load space 6
Lock adjuster nut 38
Locking clamp 33
Locking differential 57
Locking fuel filler cap 56
Locking nut 29
Locking pin 32
Lock nut
  Antilock braking 39
  Coil spring 35

Four-wheel-steering 33
  Rack and pinion 33
  Renault Clio 47
  Turbocharger 25
Lock ring 32
Lodge low-tension ignition
  coil 23
Log basket 6
Louvered hood side 51
Louvered cowling 26
Lower mount 34
Low-pressure cylinder 14
Low-profile tires 36
Lubrication 26-27
Lubrication groove 27
Lubricator 7
Lubricator sight glass 23
Luggage grid 8
Luggage rack 50

M

Macpherson strut 34
Magnet 22
Magnetic indicator
  needle 41
Magnetic fuel gauge 41
Magneto
  Ignition systems 22
  Morgan Aero 35
Mahogany casing 23
Mahogany-framed plate
  glass window 8
Mahogany-framed
  windshield 8
Mahogany-rimmed steering
  wheel 41
Main bearing 17
Main bearing housing 16
Main bevel gear 33
Main body 43
Main body cross member 52
Main body runner 52
Main casing 24
Main control harness 42
Main gear housing 30
Main journal 19
Main leaf 34
Mainplane 58-59
Main runner 31
Manual gearbox 28-29
Manual oil pump 40
Marker lamp bulb 48
Markus Motor Carriage 39
Mass production 10-11
  Cars assembled by
    hand 11
Master electrical switch 59
Master pattern 52
Mazda RX-7 18
Mechanical components of a
  Renault Clio 46-47
Mechanics 46-47
Mercedes car 31, 40-41
Mesh spring 54
Metal-studded non-skid
  tire 36
Mica insulation 23
Middle 55
Mileage recorder 40
Mirror
  Oldsmobile trim 9
  Volkswagen Beetle 13
Mirror assembly 45
Mirror reflector 45
Miter wheel 28
Mixing chamber 23
Mixture outlet 20-21
Modern engines 16-17
"Monobox" body 32
Monocoque shell 44
Morgan Aero 35
Mosquito netting 56
Mount 30
Mounting bolt 33
Mounting bracket 33
Mounting flange 20
Mounting hole 39
Mounting plate 24
Mounting point 58
Mudflap 57
Muffler
  Alvis TL 12/60 53
  de Dion-Bouton 35
  Panhard-system
    chassis 33
  Renault Clio 46
  Rolls-Royce Tourer 51
Multi-plate clutch 30-31
Multiple belt drive to rear
  axle 39

N

Natural rubber 37
Natural rubber latex 37
Neck and shoulders 55
Needle valve 20-21
NGK non-detachable plug 23

Nickel radiator 51
Nipple 37
Non-skid tire 9
Nose 23
Nose cover 59
Nylon textile cord 37

O

Observation platform 57
Observation roof hatch 57
Odometer 40-41
Offset door hinge 57
Oil bottle dripfeed 8
Oil-control ring
  Ford diesel engine 19
  Jaguar straight six
    engine 16
Oil cooler 19
Oil cooler connection 30
Oil cooler matrix 19
Oil dipstick 16
Oil drain plug 29
Oil feed 28
Oil feed pipe
  Antilock braking
    system 39
  Jaguar V12 engine 17
Oil feed to engine 58
Oil-filled lubricator 7
Oil filler 18
Oil filler cap 19
Oil filter
  Ford diesel engine 19
  Jaguar V12 engine 17
Oil float housing 52
Oil groove 15
Oil passage 19
Oil inlet 25
Oil jet 19
Oil line 35
Oil gauge 40
Oil mixed with rubber 37
Oil pick-up pipe 16
Oil pipe 24
Oil pipe banjo 17
Oil-pressure-pump body 26
Oil-pressure warning
  light 41
Oil pump
  Automatic transmission 31
  Humber engine 15
  Morgan Aero 35
Oil-pump assembly 30
Oil-pump division plate 26
Oil-pump drive 18
Oil-pump driven gear 26
Oil-pump drive shaft 26
Oil-pump front plate 26
Oil-pump housing 18
Oil-pump idler gear 26
Oil-pump idler gear
  carrier 26
Oil reservoir 31
Oil return pipe 19
Oil scavenge-pump body 26
Oil seal
  Differential unit 32
  Rotor and seals 19
Oil seal groove 19
Oil seal spring 19
Oil side lamp
  Mercedes car 31, 40
  1906 Renault 8-9
Oil sight glass 31
Oil pan
  Alvis TL 12/60 52
  Aston Martin dry sump
    26-27
  Humber engine 15
  Modern engines 16-17
Oil pan 19
Oil pick-up pipe 26
Oil supply pipe 33
Oil taillamp 31
Oil tank
  Aston Martin dry sump
    26-27
  Williams Formula One
    car 58
Oil tank filler cap 26
Oil tank filler neck 27
Oil tank mounting
  bracket 27
Oldsmobile chassis 9
Oldsmobile engine 8
Oldsmobile trim and
  bodywork 9
Oleopolymeter lubricator 23
One-way clutch 30
Openable windshield
  Ford Model T 10
  1906 Renault 9
Opera seat 9
"O"
  Gasoline fuel injection 25
  Thermostat 27
Otto cycle 14
Otto, Nikolaus 14
Outer sun wheel 32

Outer tube 34
Outlet to engine 24
Output shaft
  Manual gearbox 29
  Wankel engine 19
Output shaft flange 30
Overdrive 30
Overrider 54
Overrider support 54

P

Pad carrier 39
Pair-cast cylinder 15
Paired cylinder 14
Pan
  Alvis TL 12/60 52
  Cooling and lubrication
    26-27
  Humber engine 15
  Modern engines 16-17
Panel light control 41
Panelling
  Cars assembled by
    hand 52
  Coachbuilt cars 50
  Modern trim 48
Panhard & Levassor 28
Panhard, Rene 32
Panhard transmission
  system 32-33
Panoramic windshield 55
"Parallel" hood 51
"Park" lock wheel 30
Passenger door 13
Passenger seat 39
Pedal cluster 12
P100I electric
  headlight 43
"People's car" 12-13
Perrot shaft housing 27
Peugeot (1896) 23
Peugeot, Armand 6
Pillar
  Alvis body frame 53
  Ash frames 51
Pin 32
Pinion
  Benz Motorwagen 7
  Ford Model T 10
  Rack and pinion 33
Pinion housing
  Ford Model T 10
  Rack and pinion 33
Pinzgauer Turbo D 57-58
Pipe clip 24
Pipe connection 27
Pipe from acetylene
  generator to burner 43
Pipe to oil cooler 17
Pipe union 26-27
Piping 54
Piston
  Air conditioning pump 27
  Early engines 14-15
  Exploded disc brake 39
  Ford diesel engine 19
  Hydraulic shock
    absorber 34
  Macpherson strut 34
  Modern engines 16-17
  Power-assisted
    steering 33
  S.U. carburetor 20
  Volkswagen Beetle 12
Piston crown 17
Piston housing 39
Piston ring
  Power-assisted
    steering 33
  Trojan engine 14
Piston ring groove 17
Piston ring land 17
Piston rod
  Hydraulic shock
    absorber 34
  Steam-powered Cugnot 6
Piston skirt 17
Pivoted arm 41
Planetary gear set 30
Planet bearing 32
Planet wheel 32
Plastic jerrycan for water 56
Platform chassis 12
Platinum sparking point 23
Plenum chamber 16-17
Plug lead conduit 9
Plunger pin 37
Plywood 55
Pocketed spring 54
Pointer 40
Polybutadiene rubber 37
Poly-lacquer 55
Porcelain dome 22
Porcelain insulator 23
Porsche, Ferdinand 12
Port 24
Port for emissions
  sensor 25
Pot universal joint 35

...assisted steering 32
...assisted steering
...ck 33
...wer boosters 24-25
...ower steering belt 47
Power steering pump
  Jaguar straight six
    engine 16
  Renault Clio 47
Power steering pump
  reservoir 16
Power stroke 15
Power supply 27
Pressed steel wheel 12
Pressure gauge 56
Pressure plate 28
Primer 44
Priming cock 23
Production line
  Mass production 10
  Modern bodywork 44
  Modern trim 48
Propeller
  Ford diesel engine 19
  Turbocharger 24-25
Propeller boss 30
Drive shaft
  Four-wheel-drive running
    gear 32
  Multi-plate clutch 29
Propeller shield 30
Pull-off spring 38
Push-rod adjuster 59
Push-rod cover 52
Push-rod tube 35

Q

Quadrant 41
Quarter glass 44
Quarter panel 50-51
Quarter panel molding 48
Quarter pillar 51
Quarter trim panel 48

R

Racing car 58-59
Racing tire 59
Rack 33
Rack and pinion 33
Radial casing 36-37
Radial-ply casing 37
Radial-ply tires 36-37
Radiator air duct 59
Radiator air intake 59
Radiator and Perrot shaft
  mounting 27
Radiator apron 11
Radiator cap 26-27
  Alvis TL 12/60 52-53
  Coachbuilt cars 51
Radiator filler cap
  Ford Model T 11
  Mercedes car 40
Radiator filler neck 11
Radiator grille 57
Radiator header tank 35
Radiator hose 11
Radiators
  Alvis TL 12/60 52-53
  Coachbuilt cars 50-51
  Cooling and lubrication
    26-27
  Ford Model T 10-11
  Mercedes car 31
  Morgan Aero 35
  Panhard-system
    chassis 33
  1906 Renault 8-9
  Renault Clio 47
  Williams Formula One
    racing car 59
Radiator shell 11
Radiator stone guard 41
Radiator tank
  Alvis TL 12/60 52
  Radiators 27
Radiator tie rod 52
Radio 49
Radio aerial 57
Radio antenna
  Cadillac Eldorado 54-55
  Renault Clio 45
  Wiring harness 42
Radio speaker 49
Radius arm 31
Radius rod 10-11
Ratchet wheel 6
Rear axle
  Ford Model T 10
  Four-wheel-drive running
    gear 32
  Peugeot (1896) 23
  Rolls-Royce Tourer 51
Rear axle access 52
Rear axle bearing 10
Rear door
  Ford Model T 11

Rolls-Royce Tourer 51
Rear hatch 45
Rear lamp
  Alvis TL 12/60 53
  Oldsmobile trim 9
  Volkswagen Beetle 12
  Wiring harness 42
Rear lamps harness 42
Rear leaf spring 10
Rear oil lamp 8
Rear shelf 48
Rear shelf radio speaker 48
Rear shelf speaker 42
Rear shock absorber 12
Rearview mirror
  Cadillac Eldorado 54
  Pinzgauer Turbo D 57
  1906 Renault 8
  Renault Clio 49
  Williams Formula One
    car 59
Rebound spring 35
Recuperation chamber 34
Reduction gear case 40
Reduction gearing 41
Reflector
  Ford Model T 11
  Oldsmobile trim 9
Release handle 38
Remote linkage 29
Removable wheel 10-11
Renault (1906) 8-9
Renault Clio 44-49
Renault Espace 32
Renault logo 44
Renault V10 RS1 engine 58
Reserve oil tank 51
Retaining nut
  Drip-feed acetylene
    generator 42
  Simms magneto 22
Return spring
  Antilock braking
    system 39
  Diesel fuel injection 24
  Drum brake 38
  Weber carburetor 21
Reverse belt 31
Reverse clutch plates 30
Reverse gear 29
Reverse lever 14
Backup light 10
Reversing change-over
  switch 23
Revolution counter 40
Ribbon speedometer
  panel 41
Rigid front axle
  Leyat 30
  Panhard-system
    chassis 33
Rim
  Alvis TL 12/60 53
  Wire racing wheel 37
Rim brake 38
Rim clamp 9
Ring of felloes 36
Rivet 28
Road spring 12
Rocker arm 39
Rocker cover
  Ford diesel engine 19
  Morgan Aero 35
Rocking beam 6
Rocking lever 14
Rolls-Royce Silver Ghost "D"
  front Limousine 50-51
Rolls-Royce Silver Ghost
  Tourer 51
Roof front rail 50
Roof molding 48
Roof-rack 56-57
Roof seal 48
Roof support framing 50
Rooftop tent 56
Roof trim 48
Rotary engine 18-19
Rotary water seal 27
Rotating shaft 40
Rotor
  Rotor and seals 19
  Turbocharger 25
Rotor and seals 19
Rotor bearing 19
Rotor chamber 18
Rotor gear 18-19
Rotor journal 19
Round-corner single
  limousine coachwork 8
Round pin 7
Rubber-studded tire 36
Rub strip
  Pinzgauer Turbo D 56-57
  Renault Clio 49
Ruckstell axle 11
Rumble seat aperture rear
  corner 52
Rumble seat floor 53
Rumble seat foot well 52
Rumble seat lid 53
Rumble seat seat 53

Rumble seat side rail 52
Runner 42
Running board
  Ford Model T 11
  1906 Renault 9
  Volkswagen Beetle 13
Running board bracket
  Ford Model T 11
Running board stay 10
Running board support 11

S

Safety belts 58
Safety-gap chamber 22
Safety harness 59
Safety harness
  release 59
Safety valve 6
Safety valve weight 6
Salisbury acetylene
  headlight 43
Scott Robinson
  carburetor 21
Scraper ring 16
Screen 43
Screwdown greaser
  Mercedes car 40
  1906 Renault 8
Screwed barrel 23
Scrim 54
Scroll 50
Seal 52
Sealing "O" ring 27
Sealing plug 39
Sealing ring
  Exploded disc brake 39
  Power-assisted
    steering 33
Seat
  Alvis TL 12/60 50
  Computerized electric
    seat 42
  Daimler Maybach 31
  First cars 6-7
  Ford Model T 11
  Markus Motor Carriage 39
  Mercedes car 31
  1906 Renault 9
  Renault Clio 48-49
  Trim and upholstery
    54-55
Seat assembly 49
Seat back
  Alvis TL 12/60 50
  Daimler Maybach 31
Seat back bolster 55
Seat back rest frame 9
Seat belt
  Computerized electric
    seat 42
  Renault Clio 48-49
Seat belt catch 48
Seat belt stalk 48
Seat frame 49
Seat lift 42
Seat mount 12
Seat rake (angle) adjuster 54
Seat slide mounting
  bracket 42
Seat spring 7
Seat cushion
  Benz Motorwagen 7
  Cadillac Eldorado 55
  Oldsmobile trim 9
  Rolls-Royce Tourer 51
Sector gear 33
Securing bracket 43
Securing nut 34
Security chain 57
Semi-elliptic leaf spring
  Alvis TL 12/60 52
  Mercedes car 31
  White Steam Car 14
Sensor 22
Serrated quadrant 41
Shank 55
Shift rail 29
Shock absorber
  Aston Martin 26
  1906 Renault 8
  Renault Clio 46
  Suspension 34
  Volkswagen Beetle 12
Shoulder 36-37
Side cap 54
Side fairing 59
Side gear 19
Side harness 42
Side housing 18-19
Side lamp/Parking light
  Aston Martin 26
  Ford Model T 10-11
Side marker lamp
  Mazda RX-7 18
  Renault Clio 45
  Wiring harness 43
Side panel
  Alvis TL 12/60 53

Rolls-Royce Tourer 51
Side seal 19
Side seal groove 19
Side seal spring 19
Side steering tube 50
Side valve 15
Sidewall 36-37
Sight glass
  Mercedes car 41
  Surface carburetor 21
Sight-glass oiler 40
Sill trim 49
Silvered reflector 43
Simms high-tension
  magneto 22
Single cylinder 7
Single front driving wheel 6
Single-jet burner 43
Sipes 56
Skirt rail 53
Slat 2
Sleeve 17
Sleeve nut 24
Sleeve port 15
Sleeve valve 15
Slick racing tire 59
Sliding-pillar independent
  front suspension 35
Slip ring 22
Slot 58
Slow-running pilot jet 20
Small bevel gear 33
Small chamber 34
Snap-in valve 37
Soft trim 48
Solenoid 30
Solenoid-type fuel
  injector 25
Solex self-starting
  carburetor 20
Solid rubber tire 7
Solid tire
  Daimler Maybach 31
  Peugeot (1896) 23
Solid-tired artillery
  wheel 28
Sound-deadening rib 29
Spare tire
  Cadillac Eldorado 55
  Ford Model T 11
  Mercedes car 31
  1906 Renault 9
Spare wheel 57
Spare wheel and tire 56
Spare wheel mount 51
Spare wheel well 13
Spark gap 23
Sparking point 23
Spark plug
  Alvis TL 12/60 52
  Early engines 14-15
  Electronic ignition
    system 22
  Examples of 23
Spark plug hole 18
Spark plug lead 52
  Electronic ignition 22
  Ford V6 12-valve
    engine 16
Spark plug socket 15
Speaker and interior lamp
  harness 43
Speed and drive gear 32
Speedometer 40-41
Speedometer cable 35
Speedometer dial 40
Speed recording dial 40
Spider seat 6
Spindle 40
Spiral tubes 14
Splinter bar 7
Spoiler
  Mazda RX-7 18
  Renault Clio 45
Spoke
  Bordino Steam Carriage 7
  Wheels and tires 36-37
Spoked wheel 23
Spoke hole 36
Spool valve
  Antilock braking
    system 39
  Power-assisted
    steering 33
Sports wheel 12
Spotlight 54
Sprag brake 38
Spring 34
Spring cover 35
Spring cup 31
Spring eye
  Alvis TL 12/60 53
  Leaf spring 34
Spring hanger 31
Spring mount 35
Spring perch 10

Spring pin 34
Spring shackle
  Alvis TL 12/60 53
  Mercedes car 31
Spring shock absorber 10-11
Sprung chassis 6
Sprung seat 54
Spur wheel 28
Starter 11
Starter cog 8
Starter motor
  Renault Clio 47
  Volkswagen Beetle 12
  Wiring harness 43
Starter ring 17
Starter switch 11
Starting handle
  Aston Martin 26
  Ford Model T 10
  Panhard & Levassor 28
  Panhard-system
    chassis 33
  Peugeot (1896) 23
  1906 Renault 8-9
  White Steam Car 15
Starting handle bracket 8-9
Starting motor ring
  gear 28
Starting oiler 40
Stationary gear 18-19
Stator support shaft 31
Steam cars
  Early engines 14
  First cars 6
Steam chest 6
Steam distributor valve 6
Steam pipe 6-7
Steam-powered Cugnot
  "Fardier" 6
Steel and gunmetal spur
  wheel 28
Steel body
  Examples of spark
    plugs 23
  Pinzgauer Turbo D 56
Steel-belted radial 37
Steel belting ply 37
Steel cone 37
Steel driven gear 25
Steel nipple 37
Steel rod 37
Steel wheel
  Ford Model T 12
  Renault Clio 46-47
Steering 32-33
  Modern components 46
Steering angle input
  shaft 33
Steering arm
  Aston Martin dry sump
    26-27
  Ford Model T 10-11
  Panhard-system
    chassis 33
Steering box assembly 12
Steering cabane 30
Steering column
  Benz Motorwagen 7
  Ford Model T 11
  Renault Clio 46
  Volkswagen Beetle 13
Steering column
  connection 33
Steering connection 34
Steering gearbox 11
Steering head 7
Steering idler 12
Steering knuckle 10
Steering link
  Benz Motorwagen 7
  Williams Formula One
    car 59
Steering pump drive
  pulley 16
Steering pump pulley 16
Steering rack
  Benz Motorwagen 7
  Renault Clio 46
Steering spindle 8
Steering spindle connecting-
  rod 10
Steering tie-rod 12
Steering tiller
  Daimler Maybach 31
  First cars 6-7
  Oldsmobile trim 9
  Panhard & Levassor 28
Steering track-rod 9
Steering wheel
  Alvis TL 12/60 52
  Cadillac Eldorado 54
  Ford Model T 10-11
  Markus Motor Carriage 39
  1906 Renault 9
  Renault Clio 46, 49
  White Steam Car 14
Steering wheel rim 49
Steering wheel spider 33
Steering wiffletree 9
Step
  Panhard & Levassor 28

Steam-powered Cugnot 6
Stepper motor 33
Stepper motor bevel
  gear 33
Stepper motor wiring
  harness 33
Stereo control panel 40
Stoker's seat 6
Stoneguard 26
Stop lamp assembly 48
Storage cavity 34
Straight four cylinder
  arrangement 17
Strangler 21
Strangler lever 21
Strapontin 9
Strengthening rib 24
Stressed cylinder block 58
Strut cartridge 12
Stub axle assembly 34
Styrene-butadiene
  rubber 37
Subframe
  Panhard & Levassor 28
  Panhard-system
    chassis 33
  Renault Clio 47
S.U. carburetor
  Alvis TL 12/60 53
  Carburetors 20
Suction-regulating
  chamber 21
Sulfur 37
Sump gauze filter 27
Sump refill tank 51
Sun roof 13
Sun visor 49
Sun wheel 32
Supercharger 24-25
Support spring 54
Surface carburetor 20
Suspension 34-35
  Modern components 46
Suspension arm
  Coil and wishbone 34
  Renault Clio 46-47
Suspension push-rod 59
Suspension self-levelling
  pump 16
Suspension spring
  Coil and wishbone 34
  Renault Clio 46
Suspension strut
  Coil and wishbone 34
  Renault Clio 47
  Volkswagen Beetle 12
Suspension top mount 12
Swaged fender 50
Swaged fender 52
Swash plate
  Air conditioning
    pump 27
  Jaguar straight six
    engine 16
Swing arm 31
Swivel joint 33
Synchronizer ring 29

T

Tachometer 40
Tailgate 44
Tailgate seal 48
Tailgate support 44
Tailgate trim 48
Taillight 55
Taillight cluster 57
Tail panel 53
Tailpipe
  Volkswagen Beetle 12
  Williams Formula One
    racing car 58
Tangent-spoked wire
  wheel 7
Tank support 11
Tapered aluminum
  hood 51
Tapered needle 20-21
Tapered shaft 22
Tappet 15
Telescopic hydraulic shock
  absorber 34
Temperature-sensitive
  sticker 58
Terminal 23
Terminal nut 23
Textile-belted radial 36
Textile belting ply 36
Thermostat 27
Thread
  Hub 36
  Parts of a supercharger 25
  Wire racing wheel 37
Three-point earthed
  electrode 23
Three-quarter elliptic leaf
  spring
    de Dion-Bouton 35
    Rolls-Royce Limousine 50
Throttle arm 20

Throttle butterfly 17
Throttle cable 46
Throttle cable connection 21
Throttle lever
  Ford Model T 10
  Mercedes car 41
  Solex carburetor 20
Throttle linkage
  Jaguar V12 engine 17
  Trier and Martin
    carburetor 21
Throttle piston-valve 21
Throttle return spring 20
Throttle spindle 20-21
Throttle valve 21
Throttle-valve barrel 21
Throttle-valve lever 21
Throttle wheel 14
Thrust bearing
  Differential unit 32
  Rack and pinion 33
  Turbocharger 25
Thrust washer
  Differential unit 32
  Rack and pinion 33
Tickler 20-21
Tie 56
Tie bar 6
Tie rod
  Aston Martin dry sump
    26-27
  Elegance and utility 8-9
  Final drive and steering
    32-33
  Ford Model T 10-11
  Renault Clio 47
Tie-rod end
  Aston Martin dry sump
    26-27
  Bordino Steam Carriage 6
  Ford Model T 12
  Morgan Aero 35
  Rack and pinion 32
  Renault Clio 47
Tiger seat 6
Tiller
  Daimler Maybach 31
  First cars 6-7
  Oldsmobile trim 9
  Panhard & Levassor 28
Timing-case cover 26
Timing chain
  Humber engine 15
  Jaguar V12 engine 17
Timing chain drive
  sprocket 17
Timing cover 15
Tongue 36
Tonneau cover 55
Tool and battery box 7
Toothed wheel for speed
  sensor 30
Top cover corner block 52
Top frame
  Alvis TL 12/60 53
  Cadillac Eldorado 55
  Ford Model T 11
  Rolls-Royce Tourer 51

Top iron 6
Top mount 35
Top radiator hose 47
Top rail 51
Top support
  Alvis TL 12/60 53
  Rolls-Royce Tourer 51
Torque converter
  housing 31
Torque tube
  Ford Model T 10-11
  Rolls-Royce Tourer 51
Torsion bar 46
Torsion bar cover 12
Towing hook 7
Towing loop 57
Tow outlet 57
Track control arm 12
Trailing arm 12
Trailing brake shoe 38
Trailing spark-plug hole 18
Transaxle 12
Transfer port 14
Transmission
  Clutch and gearbox 28
  Final drive and
    steering 32
  Modern components
    46-47
  Transmission systems
    30-31
Transmission adaptor
  plate 16
Transmission casing
  de Dion-Bouton 35
  Ford Model T 11
Transmission oil pan 30
Transmission systems 30-31
Transverse leaf spring 10
Tread groove 36-37
Tread plate 57
Tread rubber 37
Trembler coil box 7
Trembler switch 23
Trier and Martin
  carburetor 21
Trilobate rotor 18
Trim 48-49, 54-55
  Oldsmobile trim 9
  1906 Renault 8-9
  Volkswagen Beetle 13
Trim of a Renault Clio 46-47
Trip odometer reset
  button 41
Trojan two-stroke engine 14
Trunk lid 55
Tubular backbone
  chassis 56
Tubular chassis 7
Tubular frame 54
"Tuck and roll" cover 54
Turbine blades 25
Turbine bypass 25
Turbine housing 25
Turbine vane 25
Turbine wheel 25
Turbocharger 24-25
  Racing cars 58
Turbo impeller 19

Turbo propeller 19
Turn signal light 43
Turn signal/parking light
  Cadillac Eldorado 54
  Pinzgauer Turbo D 57
  Volkswagen Beetle 12
Twin-cylinder engine
  Panhard-system
    chassis 33
  Steam-powered Cugnot 6
Twin-cylinder "Phoenix"
  engine 31
Twin-cylinder steam
  engine 6
Twin trailing arm
  independent front
  suspension 35
Two-burner alcohol
  stove 6
Two-jet burner 43
Types of tire 36-37
Tire carrier 9
Tire iron 56
Tire materials 37
Tire pump 56
Tires 36-37
  Alvis TL 12/60 53
  Cadillac Eldorado 54-55
  Coachbuilt cars 50-51
  First cars 6-7
  Leyat 30
  Mercedes car 31
  Panhard & Levassor 28
  Peugeot (1896) 23
  Pinzgauer Turbo D 57
  Racing cars 58-59
  1906 Renault 8-9
  Renault Clio 48-49
  Volkswagen Beetle 12
Tire security bolt 8
Tire strap 9
Tire valve 11

U

Undertray 31
Universal joint 33
Unsprung chassis 6
Untrimmed headrest 48
Upholstery 54-55
  1906 Renault 8-9
  Upholstery leathers 55
Upper flap 58
Upper mount 34

V

V12 cylinder
  arrangement 17
Vacuum actuator 25
Vacuum connection 21
Vacuum diaphragm 21
Vacuum hose 21
Valance
  Alvis TL 12/60 52-53
  Ford Model T 11

1906 Renault 9
Rolls-Royce Limousine 51
Volkswagen Beetle 13
Valve 37
Valve cover 52
Valve body 30
Valve cap
  Humber engine 15
  Snap-in valve 37
Valve core 37
Valve return spring 19
Valve rocker 16
Valve spring
  Humber engine 15
  Jaguar straight six
    engine 16
Valve stem 16
Vapor port chamber 20
Vapor space 20
Clear coat 44
Vauxhall radiator 27
V-belt pulley 19
Vee motif 54
Vent 37
Vent window 12-13
Ventilated brake disc
  (rotor) 39
Ventilation control 40
Ventilation flap 56
Vent pipe 46
Venturi (choke) 20-21
Viscous coupling 16-17
Volkswagen Beetle
  12-13
V-tube engine 23

W

Waist rail
  Alvis body frame 52
  Ash frames 51
Wankel, Felix 18
Wankel rotary cycle 18
Wankel rotary engine
  18-19
Washer jet 49
Washing bucket 57
Wastegate 25
Water bottle 47
Water chamber 42
Water connection 14
Water drain bolt 18
Water hose 52
Water inlet 27
Water jacket
  Daimler engine 15
  Ford diesel engine 19
  Humber engine 15
  Jaguar straight six
    engine 16
Water outlet 17
Water outlet
  Radiators and grilles 27
  Renault V10 RS1
    engine 58
  Thermostat 27
  Turbocharger 25

Water passage 18
Water pipe
  Humber engine 15
  Markus Motor Carriage 39
  Panhard-system chassis 33
  1906 Renault 9
Water pump
  Cooling and
    lubrication 27
  Jaguar V12 engine 17
  Renault Clio 47
  White Steam Car 14
Water pump lubricator 40
Water-pump mounting
  opening 26
Water pump pulley 19
Water rail
  Jaguar V12 engine 17
  Williams Formula One
    car 59
Water tank
  Bordino Steam Carriage 6
  Markus Motor Carriage 39
  White Steam Car 14
Water-temperature gauge
  40-41
Wax 37
Weber twin-venturi
  carburetor 21
Well-base tire 53
Welt 54
Wheelarch skirt 55
Wheelarch trim 55
Wheel bearing 34
Wheel cylinder 38
Wheel fork 7
Wheel hub
  51-52
Wheel rim 55
Wheels 36-37
  de Dion-Bouton 35
  First cars 6-7
  Ford Model T 10-11
  Leyat 30
  Markus Motor Carriage 39
  Mazda RX-7 18
  Mercedes car 31
  Panhard & Levassor 28
  Peugeot (1896) 23
  1906 Renault 9
  Renault Clio 46-47
  Volkswagen Beetle 12
Wheel spindle 35
Wheel cover 46-47, 48-49
White Steam Car 14
Whitewall tire 51
Wick 56
Wide piston-ring 14
Williams 1990 Formula One
  racing car 58-59
Wind deflector 13
Winding 22
Window blind 8
Window frame 50-51
Window glass 44
Window lift strap 8
Window washer jet 44
Window winder cable 45

Window winder handle
  Renault Clio 45, 49
  Volkswagen 13
Window winder
  regulator 13
Windshield
  Alvis TL 12/60 53
  Cadillac Eldorado 54
  Ford Model T 11
  Rolls-Royce Tourer 51
Windshield clamp 57
Windshield glass 45
Windshield heater and
  trunk light harness 42
Windshield molding 49
Windshield seal 49
Windshield stay 10
Windshield support 8
Windshield washer bottle 57
Windshield wiper 13
Windshield wiper arm 49
Windshield wiper
  blade 49
Windshield wiper bracket
  and spindles 49
Windshield-wiper motor
  assembly 12
Wing end-plate 59
Wiper arm 48
Wiper blade 48
Wiper harness 42
Wiper motor 43
Wiper switch 42
Wire framing 54
Wire gauze pad 14
Wire gauze screen 20
Wire racing wheel 37
Wire spoke 55
Wire wheel
  Leyat 30
  Wheels and tires 36
Wiring harness 42
Wishbone
  Coil and wishbone 34
  Williams Formula One
    car 59
Wooden artillery wheel 9
Wooden car frame 28
Wooden frame 6
Wooden spoke
  Bordino Steam Carriage 6
  Rolls-Royce Limousine 51
Wooden-spoked wheel 36
  Ford model T 11
  Markus Motor Carriage 39
Wooden wheel 6
Worm gear 33
Worm wheel 39
Wraparound band
  brake 38
Wraparound bumper 57
Wrist pin 17

X Y Z

Zinc phosphating 44
Zipper 56

Acknowledgments

Dorling Kindersley would like to thank the following:
Signore Amadelli, Museo dell' Automobile Carlo Biscaretti di Ruffia, for the Bordino Steam Carriage; Paul Bolton, Mazda MCL Group, for the Mazda RX-7 and the Wankel engine; Duncan Bradford of Reg Mills Wire Wheels, for the hub and wire racing wheel; John and Leslie Brewster, Autocavan, for Beetle spares; David Burgess-Wise, for the de Dion Bouton and Pilain clutch; Trevor Cass, Garrett Turbo Service, for the turbocharger; John Corbett, The Patrick Collection, for the Jaguar V12 engine; Gary Crumpler, Williams Grand Prix Engineering Ltd, for the Grand Prix car and engine; Mollie Easterbrooke and Duncan Gough, Overland Ltd, for the Pinzgauer Turbo D; Arthur Fairley, Vauxhall Motor Company, for the digitized instrument panel; Paul Foulkes-Halbard, Filching Manor Motor Museum, for the 70HP Mercedes and the Oldsmobile; Frank Gilbert, I. Wilkinson and Son Ltd, for the Rolls-Royce Silver Ghost "D" front limousine, the 1913 and 1924 Rolls-Royce Silver Ghost Tourers, the Alvis TL 12/60, and the Lanchester chassis; Paolo Gratton, Gratton Museum, for the Ford Model T; Colvin Gunn, of Gunn & Son, for the supercharger; Judy Hogg of Ecurie Bertelli, for the Aston Martin; Milton Holman, Dream Cars, for the Cadillac; Ian Matthews, IMAT Electronics, for assistance; Eric Neal, Jaguar Cars Ltd, for the Jaguar engines, fascia, sectioned seat, and running gear, and for general assistance; Paul Niblett, Keith Davidson, Mark Reumel, and David Woolf, Michelin Tyre plc, for tyres and materials; Doug Nye, for assistance; Kevin O'Keefe, O'Keefe Cars, for the electric seat; Seat UK, for the Seat Ibiza; Roger Smith, for the Leyat; Jim Stirling, Ironbridge Gorge Museum, for the wooden wheel; Jon Taylor, for the Beetle; Doug Thompson, for the sprung seat; and Martyn Watkins, Ford Motor Company Ltd. In particular, for invaluable assistance and the supply of many items for photography: The National Motor Museum, Beaulieu; Alf Newell, Renault UK Ltd; David Suter, Cheltenham Cutaway Exhibits Ltd; and Francesca Riccini, Science Museum.

Additional photography:
Michelangelo Gratton of Vision, Peter Chadwick, Dave King, Nick Parfitt.

Additional editorial assistance:
Roger Tritton, Fiona Courtney-Thompson, Deirdre Clark.